How to **Talk** to **Teens** About **Really Important Things**

Specific Questions and Answers and Useful Things to Say

Charles E. Schaefer, Ph.D.

Theresa Foy DiGeronimo, M.Ed.

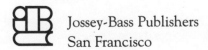

Jossey-Bass Publishers
San Francisco

The list of positive reasons to participate in athletics from *Myth Busting: What Every Female Athlete Should Know!* is reprinted by permission of the Women's Sports Foundation. Copyright © 1997 by the Women's Sports Foundation.

The list of common cult recruiter characteristics from *How Can Young People Protect Themselves Against Cults?* is reprinted by permission of the American Family Foundation.

Jossey-Bass books and products are available through most bookstores. To contact Jossey-Bass directly, call (888) 378-2537, fax to (800) 605-2665, or visit our website at www.josseybass.com.

Substantial discounts on bulk quantities of Jossey-Bass books are available to corporations, professional associations, and other organizations.

For details and discount information, contact the special sales department at Jossey-Bass.

 Manufactured in the United States of America on Lyons Falls Turin Book. This paper is acid-free and 100 percent totally chlorine-free.

Library of Congress Cataloging-in-Publication Data

Schaefer, Charles E.
    How to talk to teens about really important things: specific questions and answers and useful things to say / Charles E. Schaefer and Theresa Foy DiGeronimo. — 1st ed.
        p. cm.
    ISBN 0-7879-4358-4 (paper: alk. paper)
    1. Teenagers—United States—Attitudes. 2. Teenagers—United States—Conduct of life. 3. Questions and answers—United States. I. DiGeronimo, Theresa Foy. II. Title.
HQ796 .S37 1998
305.235—ddc21   98-40078

FIRST EDITION
PB Printing   10 9 8 7 6 5 4 3 2

Acknowledgments

We would like to thank our editor, Alan Rinzler, for recognizing the need for this book. His editorial insights and personal experiences have added much to the quality of the book.

For their insights on ethics, moral values, and religion, we would like to thank youth ministers Fred Mercadante (Chatham, New Jersey) and Glen McCall (Pompton Lakes, New Jersey).

For helping us prepare "Competition," we thank David Feigley, director of youth sport research, Rutgers University, New Brunswick, New Jersey.

For sharing his experience and knowledge about cults, we thank Michael Langone, Ph.D., editor of *Cultic Studies Journal* and executive director of America's Family Foundation.

For giving us research and information on cults, we thank Nelson Baez (South Plainfield, New Jersey).

For her store of knowledge and her willingness to help, we thank Lorraine Powell, substance awareness coordinator at Hawthorne High School, Hawthorne, New Jersey.

Contents

Part Three: Concerns of Teens 137

To my children, Karine and Eric,
who throughout their adolescence made our family talks
an enjoyable challenge.
C.E.S.

To my children, Matt, Joe, and Colleen,
who are always there to make me practice what I preach.
T.F.D.

Introduction

How often do you really talk and listen to your teenager? A 1998 *USA Weekend* survey of 272,400 students asked how often they have a conversation that lasts longer than fifteen minutes with a parent. Only a third said daily. About one in five (17 percent) said they almost never talk to their parents for more than fifteen minutes. A third said adults generally don't value their opinion. Another 1998 nationwide poll of thirteen- to seventeen-year-olds conducted by the *New York Times* and CBS News found that 55 percent of the teens agreed that there were times when they had something they wanted to talk to their parents about but did not do so. Of these, four out of five said the reason was that their parents "won't understand," and most of the rest said their parents were simply too busy.

What would your teen say? How often do you talk to your teenagers? How often do they come to you with important questions and issues? We have written this book to help bridge the gap in parent-teen communication. In each chapter, we have put together a unique collection of advice, information, and sample dialogues that are based on years of clinical practice, parental experience, and scholarly research. We hope this book will be a valued resource in the years to come when you talk to your teens about their experiences and help them through crises.

1

We don't pretend that there are easy answers to the difficult problems of adolescence, but we do believe that talking about them can help. We also don't pretend that one book can tell you exactly what to say in every situation or even that teenagers will listen to everything you tell them. Still, it is important to inform them of the facts and the ideals that make for a better life. Whether they admit it or not, teens like to hear what you expect of them. They like to know that you care enough to try and that you love them enough to keep talking even when it seems they've slammed the door shut.

We realize, of course, that every family situation is unique. (We know that in addition to so-called traditional parents, there are gay parents, foster parents, adoptive parents, grandparents, working parents, and guardians.) So we want to say right here in the beginning that nothing in this book should be considered gospel or the "only best way." We are sure, however, that the guidelines we suggest can be adapted to fit your family's belief system and lifestyle and give you a strong base from which to build open and honest communication.

WHY SHOULD YOU TALK TO YOUR KIDS?

Teenagers will eventually find the answers to all their questions—but from whom? If you want to be their primary source of information, let them know that right from the start by talking to them openly, matter-of-factly, and honestly about the many issues that are important in their lives.

Strive to be an "askable" parent—that is, someone your teens feel will not judge, tease, or punish them for asking questions about really important topics. An askable parent responds to questions with words and actions that say, "I'm so glad you asked."

Teenagers intuitively sense how receptive you are to talking about certain subjects. If you avoid talking about emotionally sensitive topics like death, prejudice, or divorce, they learn to keep their concerns to themselves. If you ignore "embarrassing" issues like pornography, homosexuality, and sexually transmitted diseases, your teens will get their information (or misinformation) from someone else. If you slight the importance of such life experiences as tattoos, body piercing, date rape, or school violence, your teens will assume you just don't understand their concerns and fears.

Open communication is a most powerful parenting tool; the information in this book will help you use it often and wisely.

HOW TO TALK TO YOUR KIDS

The way you talk to teens is as important as what you say. Each chapter suggests specific guidelines appropriate for the given topic. But always keep in mind these ground rules:

Know What You're Talking About. To be effective in giving advice or counsel, you have to establish yourself in the eyes of your teen as someone who is informed. So before offering advice on such topics as sex or alcoholism, you should read up on these topics. At the end of most chapters, you'll find a suggested reading list for parents and teens. Read through some of these books, *before* you broach the subject with your kids. Your opinion will be more credible if you offer supporting evidence instead of just stating your view.

Be Trustworthy. Be forthright about what you know and honest about what you don't know. Avoid exaggerating the truth to make an impression or distorting the truth to spare your teen or yourself discomfort. Let your children learn that they can trust what you tell them.

Be Brief. Don't beat around the bush; get right to the point. You will keep your teen's attention and respect if you can avoid the tendency to give a lecture or a lengthy, involved argument.

Be Clear. Use simple, concrete language geared to your teen's level of development.

Respect Your Child's View. Ask your teens what they think about issues rather than just telling them what to do or think. Remember to listen to and respect your teen's opinions so that you talk *with* them rather than *at* them. Respect also involves giving teenagers reasons for behaving in a certain way. Reasons help develop a teen's thinking powers and independence of judgment.

Why you should talk with your teens, *when* you should talk, and *how* you should talk are what this book is all about. We won't argue, debate, or lecture on the many controversial theories and practices inherent in some of the topics. We strive solely to give you the words you need to talk to your kids about really important subjects—subjects our grandparents and even our parents thought too private, insignificant, or taboo to mention.

As a team, we have written eight parenting books (several of which have been translated into other languages and published internationally). We are delighted to offer you this ninth one. We know firsthand that talking to kids can sometimes be difficult, awkward, and even frustrating, but we also know that the end result is well worth the effort. If you talk to your teenagers often and openly about any subject in the world, they'll quickly learn that they can trust you with their secrets and fears. As they grow, this trust will enrich your relationship and encourage them to look to you, not the streets, for the information they need to stay safe and healthy. With this goal in mind, we hope this book will become a trusted resource that you can pull out on all those days down the road when you'll need to find just the right words to talk to your kids about really important things.

If you ever feel frustrated in your efforts to talk to your teens, keep in mind that it's quite normal for teenagers to believe they already know it all. It was Mark Twain who observed that when he was seventeen, he thought his father to be the stupidest man in the world. When Twain was twenty-one, he was amazed how much this man had learned in four short years. Have patience and keep trying.

December 1998

Charles E. Schaefer
Hackensack, New Jersey

Theresa Foy DiGeronimo
Hawthorne, New Jersey

Part One

Major Crises

Divorce

There had been no laughter in fifteen-year-old Mike's home for a long time. He couldn't remember the last time he saw his mother smile. But still, he couldn't believe that his parents were really going to get a divorce. Maybe it was just another argument that they'd get over. Maybe his father would move back in on the weekend. Or maybe he wouldn't even see him this week; maybe he'd never see him again. Maybe his mother would want to move. Maybe they couldn't afford college now. "I hate both of them," Mike thought. "How could they do this to me?"

Getting divorced is not what Mike's parents had "done to him." Mike knows divorce happens to lots of families—every year, another million children see their parents split up. What his parents did that hurts so much was to leave him with so many unanswered questions.

Parents are generally very sensitive to the effects of divorce on young children. The effect of this family crisis on teenagers, however, is often overlooked. Teens, it is sometimes erroneously assumed, are so involved in their own lives and are so infrequently at home that they are not terribly affected by their parents' divorce. The truth is, adolescents need as much emotional and behavioral guidance during this time of crisis as a child at any other stage of development. We believe their need for help is particularly urgent for two reasons: (1) they are just beginning to build their own image of the male-female relationship, which can be shaken by a family divorce, and (2) their methods of acting out their anger and sadness include dangerous, life-changing options such as alcohol, drugs, sex, and school failure.

There's no doubt that teens have lots of questions to ask and a heart full of feelings to work out when they discover their parents are separating. They need to talk to someone who can listen to their perspective, someone who can listen calmly and without judgment, someone who can encourage ongoing dialogues. We hope this someone will be you.

WHY TALK TO TEENS ABOUT DIVORCE

There are a thousand reasons to talk to your teenage children about your divorce. The following are a few of the most common ones:

• *A teen's maturity level.* A teen's newly assumed independent attitude fools many parents into thinking that they can handle a divorce better than a young child might. But often the opposite is true. Because they are mature, teens can't be talked out of their emotions with promises of lollipops; they can't be fooled by a parent's smile. They are very aware of everything that's going on and need to be involved in family discussions that show respect for their role in the family dynamics.

• *Normal anxieties.* The teen years are full of insecurities, worries, and anxieties in even the best of circumstances. These feelings are all heightened by divorce, and they need to be talked about so that they do not become overwhelming.

• *Shattered expectations*. Teenagers are forming their first strong emotional attachments to the opposite sex and are beginning to fantasize about living happily ever after with their own mate. This makes the divorce of a parent especially shattering if there is no dialogue that offers a calm and understanding look at the situation.

• *Hidden feelings*. Some teens wear a mask of aloofness and try to hide their real feelings about everything. They won't ask questions they are dying to have answers to. They won't bring up any subject they think is sensitive for their parents. They tend to stay very quiet. In this time of crisis, this attitude becomes especially difficult to wear for very long. Hidden feelings may trigger problems with schoolwork or with siblings. They may push a teen into risky behaviors like substance abuse or promiscuity. Talking openly and honestly helps teens put aside their masks and let out the emotions that hurt so much when held inside.

• *Mixed feelings*. Many teens are very aware of why their parents are divorcing. They have been living in the same house and have heard all the arguments and withstood the icy atmosphere. They may respond to the news of a divorce with initial relief. But don't let this reaction fool you into thinking there's nothing more to be said. Even teens who can understand the need for the divorce may still need help coping with occasional feelings of betrayal, anger, disillusionment, and sadness.

• *Emotional well-being*. Some teens protect themselves from pain by turning off their feelings. They don't feel the pain of your divorce, but they also don't feel joy or happiness in life. They become emotional zombies. Without a chance to talk about feelings, the psychological damage can be long lasting and affect the quality of a teen's life long after the crisis is past.

WHEN TO TELL YOUR KIDS
ABOUT YOUR DIVORCE DECISION

Your children should be told of your decision to separate and pursue a divorce when a final irrevocable decision has been made. Once you're sure the marriage is over, following these guidelines will help you choose the right time to talk to your children about this decision:

Talk When Both Parents Can Be Together. When both parents sit down and give the news, kids are more likely to accept the finality of the decision. If only one parent breaks the news, the teens may think there was an argument and that the other parent will soon be back to make up. Telling your kids about a divorce decision together also lessens the possibility that they will hear two completely different stories or confusing contradictions from each parent.

If your spouse can't be there when you break the news, arrange for him or her to call or write your children almost immediately after your talk. Whenever possible, kids need to hear this information from both parents. If, however, your spouse is totally unavailable due to disappearance, mental illness, hostility, withdrawal, or the like, you'll have to handle the discussion alone. In this case, you can explain (without anger or judgment) your spouse's silence by saying something like, "Your dad [mom] is unable to talk to you about this right now. But I'm here any time you want to talk."

Talk When You're at Home. Don't break this news in public—at the park, in a restaurant, or the like. And don't tell your kids at a time when you or they have to be out the door for work or school. Give them time to absorb your announcement, ask questions, cry if they want, and look for assurances in your hug.

Talk When You've Attained a Sense of Calm. No matter how angry or upset you may be about the breakup of your marriage, don't dump your emotional load on your kids. Certainly, you can share your feelings of sadness and upset, but try to stay calm.

Talk When All Siblings Are Together. The presence of siblings can cushion the shock and provide a sense of family continuity. It also gives your children permission to turn to each other for support. You may want to speak to older children alone to offer a more detailed explanation, but the initial announcement should be made with the whole family present.

Talk over Time. Your teen's initial reaction to your divorce plans will require a particular response, but over time you can expect the reaction to change, and you need to keep up your dialogue through each stage. It is not uncommon after the separation to see a child go through the same stages of grief you would expect after the death of a loved one. You should watch for each of the following stages (based on the grief work of Elisabeth Kübler-Ross) and listen to your teen's feelings at each and every stage:

Denial (You'll get back together.)
Anger (You've ruined my life.)
Bargaining (I promise I won't argue with you any more if you and Dad [Mom] try one more time.)
Depression (Life just stinks.)
Acceptance (I guess it's for the best.)

These feelings don't usually happen on schedule or even in order. Your teen may bounce back and forth from one to the other. It may take years before she reaches the acceptance stage (usually in late teens). It's difficult to keep track of your teen's changing feelings (especially when you're on your own emotional roller-coaster). But it is so important to stay attentive and try to be under-standing and empathic. When your teens yells, "I hate you!" you can guess she's in the "angry" stage. This makes it a bit easier to respond with love.

WHAT TO TALK ABOUT

How you decide what words you use when you break the news will depend on all the factors surrounding your impending divorce. Many parents simply say:

"I'm sure you know that Mom [Dad] and I are not happy living together. We have decided that it is best if we get a divorce and live apart. We wanted to tell you this now so that as we go through the proceedings and things start to change around here, you'll know what's going on. We'll try to keep you informed about our decisions about things like who's moving where and when, but if you have any questions we're not answering, be sure to ask us."

After you initially break the news, your child may become very quiet and need time alone to sort out her feelings, or she may have a hundred immediate questions. It's also possible that your teen will get very angry very quickly. Whatever the reaction, you must stay calm and accepting. This is not a time to teach good manners or expect courtesy.

Information
It's easy to get so caught up in your own world during a divorce that you forget to pass on information to your kids. Although it's under-

standable that you are distracted, it's also understandable that your teen will handle the divorce better if he's up-to-date about what's going on. When you break the news, be straightforward. Teenagers should be informed of the impending separation in an honest, direct manner—no lies, no excuses, no false promises. Stating the situation firmly and without hesitation will convey the finality of the decision. Teenage children expect their parents to solve problems and be responsible adults. If you are not clear and straightforward, they will hold out hope that you will get back together, or they may be angry that you haven't tried hard enough. Tell your teen:

"All reasonable alternatives have been considered, and there is no other solution possible."

Teenagers have a passion for knowing the truth and have a nose for sniffing it out. You can't fool them for very long. Your teen may already know the reasons for your divorce, or you may need to explain your decision. Either way, you do not need to reveal all the sordid details of things like infidelity, substance abuse, and alienation. If your teens push you for more detailed explanations than you think is appropriate, you can tell them:

"This information is personal and private and just between parents."

Take the focus away from the reasons for the divorce and put it on your children by telling them:

"Our decision to separate will have an effect on you, so we wanted to talk to you about what's going to happen."

This is, after all, what most interests your child. Teens understand such concepts as custody, child support, and property division. You should be very open about how these arrangements will affect your children. They will want to know:

"Which parent will I live with?"
Too many parents feel their teens are old enough to decide which parent they would like to live with and hand them the responsibility for choosing. This puts kids in a very disturbing position. Unless the child needs to flee an abusive situation, no son or daughter should ever be asked to choose. No matter which choice he makes he will live with terrible guilt for not choosing the other. (This is often the case even when the teen has a strong preference.) If the parents cannot make the decision (keeping the teen's preference in mind), a mediator or judge can decide. Whenever possible, a teen's preference should be honored, but the teen should not be the one who makes the final pronouncement.

"Will I see the other parent? When? Who will set up the schedule?"
Don't assume your teen knows she will see the noncustodial parent again. Tell her and give her the details. Offer reassurances that there will be continued contact. Make sure you involve your teen in mapping out the details. Teenagers live very active lives, and getting together with their friends on a Saturday afternoon may be much more important than visiting with the noncustodial parent. Ask for input before making up a schedule.

"Will I have to move or change schools?"
This is a big issue for teenagers. If he has to move, be up front and say so as soon as the decision is made. Sure, he may not like it, but don't hold it as a surprise until the last possible moment. We all need time to adjust to upcoming major life changes. Conversely, try not to worry your kids with moving plans that aren't definite. It's

emotionally disturbing to be "teased" with plans that change from day to day.

"Will we have enough money?"
Teenagers are smart enough to know that a divorce often affects the flow of money in the house. Be honest with your kids about how things will change or not change. If you'll have to budget more carefully for a while, tell them and ask for their help and understanding. But then drop it; try not to make moaning over financial problems the focus of all your dinner conversations. Many teens have a flair for the melodramatic and will imagine themselves homeless and starving if their parents complain too much about money problems.

These questions and answers focus on the ways the divorce will directly affect your teens. That's what they want and need to know. They should not be burdened with the financial and legal details of your divorce, so be careful not to give them more information than they can (or should have to) handle.

Emotional Stability
In addition to information, your teen needs to know where she stands in the new family arrangement. One question that will bother your teen is the problem of changing roles. Too often, divorcing parents look to their teenage children for things they are not prepared or able to give. Suddenly they are asked to be a mediator, a confidant, a go-between, or a sounding board. You can give your teen emotional stability if you make an effort to keep your relationship after the divorce on the same level as before the divorce. Don't push her into roles she doesn't belong in. Don't ask her to listen to your problems. Don't ask her to deliver messages to your partner. Tell your teen:

"You are my daughter [son], and that's all I expect you to be during this difficult time."

Avoid criticizing your partner to your child. If you and your partner are involved in a particularly hostile divorce, tell your children that you are both feeling very angry and upset with each other and that things may not be so pleasant around the house for a while. Say:

"Your father [mother] really makes me angry. But my anger has nothing to do with you. I may be in a bad mood a lot, but I love you, and your father [mother] loves you. This is between us."

Assure your teen that the divorce-related problems are strictly between you and your partner. Say:

"We have not made this decision because of anything you have done. You are not at all responsible. I want you to know that we don't expect you to choose sides."

Even in situations where the teen knows life will be better after the divorce (especially in cases of abuse), she may still have periods of anger and hostility. Try to understand these emotions.

Don't say: "I thought you understood why I had to get a divorce! Why are you getting angry now?"
Instead, say: "Even when divorce is the best solution, I know it still hurts."

Safety
Divorce can make teens feel lost and drifting without a home base—this is a frightening feeling. To balance this feeling, teens need to be told, and told again, that both their parents love them. Say:

"Your father [mother] and I love you very much. That's the hardest part of the divorce—knowing that it hurts you. But I want you to know that you'll always have a safe place to live and all our love."

Some teens find it hard to openly express their feelings about divorce. If this happens, you can initiate conversation by saying something like:

"Sometimes I feel upset about the divorce. Do you ever feel that way?"

"Have you noticed how things have changed around here since your father left?"

"What's it like for you going back and forth between here and your mother's place?"

Don't push too hard for a response, but keep offering your sympathetic shoulder. If repeatedly given the opportunity, most children will eventually talk about what's on their mind.

When they do talk, the first thing you should do is listen. Don't try to straighten out misconceptions. Don't give your opinion. Let your teen finish before you jump in. Try to see what she is saying from her point of view. Don't assume you know what she is feeling or what she thinks. Let her get it all out. You'll find it much easier to talk about the facts of your divorce if your teen believes you will listen to her view of the situation.

RESPONSES TO WATCH FOR

If your teens are very upset by your divorce, they may express their hurt in a number of ways. Watch for any of the following and be aware that each response may be a cry for attention and help.

Sadness

Sorrow can be very loud, or it can be silent. Your teens may cry a lot, or they may become lethargic or withdrawn. If you ask, "What's the matter?" they'll pull away or sadly report, "Oh, nothing *(sigh)*." This mental malaise can affect a child's ability to concentrate and will therefore influence school achievement. If you notice behavioral changes in your teens, it's probably best to tell their teachers about the divorce. Teachers can become supportive allies if they know the reasons for sudden moodiness or behavior problems.

Anger

Anger has many faces. Older children are developing a strict sense of right and wrong—a divorce seems "wrong." Fifteen-year-old Jack, for example, showed his anger in his irritable response to anything his mother said. If his mom asked simply, "What do you want for breakfast?" Jack would snap, "What do you care? All you care about is yourself," and then stomp out of the room.

Passive Aggression

Passive aggression allows a teen to be angry and lash out without making a sound. Thirteen-year-old Kelly, for example, never spoke harshly to her dad after he moved out of the house, but instead chose to ignore his presence. She pretended she didn't hear anything her father said. She purposely would "forget" she was supposed to be home for a visit. She would "accidentally" hang up the receiver if her dad called on the phone. Teens who do this are not being intentionally rude; they're feeling angry.

Escape

If the divorce is particularly loud and upsetting, your teen may choose to escape from the whole scene. Escape can take many forms, including staying away from the house, emotional withdrawal, school failure, drug and alcohol abuse, and sexual promiscuity.

YOUR RESPONSE

It's best to handle the reactions of teens with lots of understanding and support. Although you should maintain whatever form of discipline you used before the separation, try to be patient with your teens as they adjust to their new family situation. Allow your teens to express their feelings openly—many feelings and actions serve as defenses against pain and grief. What you can do is recognize the cause of the emotion and always keep your door open.

If you notice dangerous behaviors like substance abuse, school failure, or sexual promiscuity, your teen needs immediate psychological intervention.

The following general do's and don'ts will help your teen talk about your divorce decision.

Do's

- Encourage your teens to verbalize their feelings (even the hurtful angry ones) and give them opportunities to ask questions.
- Listen closely to their concerns.
- Discourage teens' wishful thinking that this will blow over and that soon they will have both parents together again in a happy home (even if this is your own wish).
- Remember that one conversation about the details of the divorce is not enough. Repeated conversations give teens the chance to digest the painful news and accept the reality of it.
- Repeatedly assure your children that the divorce is not their fault.

- Tell your children that both parents love them now and always will.
- Keep your teen informed about divorce-related events and decisions that affect them.

Don'ts

- Don't be indecisive. If the divorce is going to happen, say so firmly, allowing no room for leeway.
- Don't blame your former spouse for the breakup (even if the fault is clearly on one side).
- Don't bad-mouth your former spouse in front of your children.
- Don't ever ask your teens to choose sides.
- Don't look to your children for emotional support.
- Don't discourage expression of emotions by saying things like, "Don't cry. I need you to be strong."
- Don't try to minimize the loss with comments like, "Oh, you never saw your father much anyway."

GETTING HELP

It's understandable if you find yourself in too much emotional pain of your own to give your teen the attention he or she needs. But it's essential, especially in the middle of the crisis period, that you make plans to address the needs of your child. Mediation is one path that may help your family through the pain of divorce. This process gives you the power to make your own decisions, and it offers both partners the opportunity to meet with a trained, neutral third party, who helps you discuss issues, concerns, and differences in a nonadversarial setting. The mediation process can help you focus on your child's needs and help you explore various ways to resolve your differences. Mediation attempts to reduce the hostility between parents and to bring about a more positive outcome for children. If you have the opportunity to engage in divorce mediation, we recommend it highly.

You and your child may also benefit from psychological counseling to prevent problems from occurring. A trained family therapist can help both of you understand your feelings and come to terms with what life has handed you.

RESOURCES

American Association for Marriage and Family Therapy
1100 17th Street N.W.
Washington, DC 20036
(800) 374-2638

This organization can refer you to therapists in your local area who specialize in counseling families of divorce.

Divorce Anonymous
2600 Colorado Avenue, Suite 270
Santa Monica, CA 90404
(310) 998-6538

These groups are located primarily in western states. They provide emotional support and information to divorcing families.

FOR FURTHER READING

Bienenfeld, Florence. *Helping Your Child Through Your Divorce*. Alameda, Calif.: Hunter House, 1994.

Especially for Teens

Johnson, Linda Carlson. *Everything You Need to Know About Your Parents' Divorce*. (2nd ed.) New York: Rosen Publishing Group, 1992.

Kimball, Gayle. *How to Survive Your Parents' Divorce: Kids' Advice to Kids*. Chico, Calif.: Equality Press, 1994.

Levine, Beth. *Divorce: Young People Caught in the Middle*. Springfield, N.J.: Enslow, 1995.

Death of
a **Loved One**

Sixteen-year-old Jennifer answered the phone in the kitchen when it rang early one Sunday morning. Her parents heard her familiar cheerful voice greet her best friend, May. Then they heard a scream and rushed to find Jennifer rolled up in a ball crying hysterically on the floor. "No! No!" Jennifer kept yelling. "No. It can't be true."

Jennifer had just received the tragic news that two of her classmates had died in a car crash the night before. What can her parents say to ease this kind of pain? What can they do?

UNDERSTANDING THE
EMOTIONAL STRAIN OF DEATH ON TEENS

Talking to teens about death can be especially difficult because there is a gap between what they know intellectually and what they feel in their hearts. Cognitively, teens know how death works—it is universal, inevitable, and irreversible. Unfortunately, adults often assume that this knowledge is all teens need to handle the death of

a loved one. But just because a teen can deal with death intellectually doesn't mean he is emotionally mature enough to deal with his
feelings of loss. Emotionally, teens are living in a life stage that is
tumultuous to begin with—they constantly shift back and forth
between being independent and being dependent. Death makes this
uncertain time even more difficult to handle. Should they be independent and strong by not crying or reaching out? Or should they
run back to the arms of their family for comfort? They don't know.
Teens need an empathic adult to help them understand their own
emotions and to pass through the stages of grief.

Death comes into a teen's life in many forms. It may take a
beloved grandparent. It may happen unexpectedly to a parent, sib-
ling, or friend. It may happen through a suicide or violent act. It
may happen after an accident or a long illness. Each event carries
with it unique heartache and family dialogues that can't be prescribed in any book. But there are some general statements you can
make to help your teens deal with the feelings of loss after death.
These are described in this chapter.

SPEAK THROUGH EXAMPLE

Your teen may look to you to decide how to handle death. If you too
are mourning, show your feelings and share your emotions with your
teen. Let him know that you too feel angry, or sad, or exhausted, or
whatever. If you feel like crying, go ahead. Keeping up a brave front
"for the sake of the children" is a mistake that teaches them to hide
their own feelings.

Talk about your feelings. Share your feelings with your teens.
Don't shut them out. If you act honestly, openly, and lovingly, your
teens may take your cue and respond the same way.

If you feel that your own grief is keeping you from supporting your teen, ask for help. Ask relatives, close friends, or your family minister, priest, or rabbi to talk with your teen and let him know that people care and understand his need for support.

USE SILENCE AND UNDERSTANDING TO TALK ABOUT DEATH

Many teens will go through a very typical pattern of mourning by saying and doing things that are not rational or realistic. This is not a good time to try to convince them of the "truth." In the time shortly after the death of a loved one, your best communication strategy will be to listen to what your teen says and respond, not to redirect his feelings but to confirm them and offer understanding through each of the typical stages of grief:

Stage 1: Denial
Your teen may feel numb and insist:

> "He can't be gone."
> "This is just a dream."
> "I don't believe it."

Don't say: "You have to accept it. These things happen."
Instead, listen and then try: "It does seem too awful to be true. I can't believe it either."

Stage 2: Hostility
Your teen may lash out:

> "There is no God."
> "Nobody else understands how I feel!"
> "It doesn't pay to be good."

Don't say: "Don't talk like that. That's not true."
Instead, listen and then try: "I know you're very angry right now. You have a right to be."

Stage 3: Depression

Your teen may feel that he can't cope with his feelings of sadness:

"I can't go on without him."
"I don't want to live without him."
"I feel so empty and lonely."

Don't say: "Of course you will go on. You have to. Don't talk like that. You're scaring me."
Instead, listen and then try: "Death is very hard to accept. Sometimes we feel like we don't want to go on anymore. But I promise you this feeling will pass, and you'll see that your life will go on, and you will feel happy again one day."

Stage 4: Acceptance

Eventually your teen will come to accept death. She will find that she can remember the deceased without pain. She'll realize that she can remember him and still be happy. She will have learned that life goes on. But this takes time; six months to a year is an average period of mourning, so have patience with your teen as she tries to deal with the pain that accompanies death. Your silence while you listen and your understanding when you respond will be of great comfort.

COMMON REACTIONS TO GRIEF

As your teen travels through the various stages of mourning, you may notice several uncharacteristic behaviors that cry out for your attention.

Exhaustion

When all your energy is used up on the emotional job of dealing with grief, walking up the stairs can suddenly become too tiresome a chore. Your teen may sleep much of the time (which also helps make the pain go away); he may sit around listlessly; he may not have enough energy to get back into daily activities like schoolwork or even dinner table conversation.

Don't say: "All right, that's enough moping. It's time to get on with living. I want you to cheer up and get out of your room today."
Instead, try: "I've noticed that you need to be alone and quiet lately. This probably is helping you sort out your feelings and come to grips with your loss. But I want you to know that when you do want to talk, I'm a very good listener. I'd be happy to hear what you think about Dan's death. I'd like you to share with me what he meant to you."

Hyperactivity

Some mourners jump into high gear. They mourn by hopping from one activity to another, never stopping to think or reflect. They may talk incessantly about nothing and appear to be a bundle of nervous energy. This teen is trying to avoid her inward thoughts of death that bring such pain, and she may also be trying to avoid an outward display of emotions by staying busy and strong. You can help a hyperactive teen stop and face what she's running from by talking about the deceased.

Try: "Funny, but today Dan was on my mind a lot. I kept thinking about all the things you two did together. Do you have a favorite memory of him?"

If your teen still refuses to talk, you can gently encourage her to respect her feelings and let them out.

You might say: "It seems to me that you're afraid to show how you really feel about Dan's death. You shouldn't try to be brave, because unexpressed grief stays with you; it doesn't go away. You have to let it out to get over it. A good friend once told me, 'You can't go around grief. You have to go through it.' So if you want to talk about Dan, I'd like to listen."

Fear

Some young mourners become very fearful. Reacting to the concrete reminder of mortality, they worry that they too will soon die. They become afraid to be alone at night; they live with a sense of panic that they can't explain. They thought they were invincible, and now they must confront the possibility of death.

Don't say: "Just because Dan died doesn't mean you're going to die. Don't be silly. Now come on, stop worrying so much."

Instead, try: "It's very common for people to become fearful after the death of a loved one. I think death makes us all very aware of our own mortality. But I want you to know that I'm always here to support and help you until this feeling passes—and it will go away in time."

Anger

There's a lot to be angry about after the death of a loved one. Your teen may be angry at the doctor for not being able to save the life; at friends for the way they talk about the death; at family members for not understanding how tragic death is; at the dead person for dying; at himself for feeling so out of control. All this anger comes out in ways that may seem uncharacteristic of your child. There may be sudden fights with siblings; there may be outbursts at school;

there may be violent arguments with you. It's difficult for even the most understanding parent to put up with this misdirected anger.

Don't say: "I've had it with you. I know you're angry about Dan's death, but you can't keep yelling at me. I did not kill him; I had nothing to do with what happened. So you have to stop being angry at me!"

Instead, try: "I know you're feeling very angry, but I think the anger has more to do with your grief over Dan's death than how you feel about me. I'd like to help you get rid of some of that anger. I've read that a good way to release pent-up anger is to do something physical. The next time you feel like exploding, why don't you take your pillow and bang it against your bed for a while, or you could take the dog for a run, or how about chopping some wood [or scrubbing floors or whatever]? You need to be able to express your anger without hurting the people you love. I think it also might help if we talk about Dan; talking may help you see what it is you're angry about."

Guilt

Guilt is an emotion that is directed inward. It can make it much harder for your teen to grieve and get past the pain of death. Teens feel guilty about death when they get it in their heads that they could have somehow prevented it. "If only I made my dad give up smoking." "If only I had been at the party, I wouldn't have let Dan get in the car with someone who was drinking." "If only I had talked to Grandma more often." "If only. . . ." Sometimes the guilt has some basis in fact, and sometimes it is irrational, but either way, your teen needs to get past it.

Don't say: "Don't be ridiculous. You had absolutely nothing to do with Dan's death. Stop thinking like that."

Instead, try: "When someone we're close to dies, we tend to think of things we might have done to prevent it or things we would have liked to have done or said. But since we're not God, and we don't know for certain when people will die, it's not fair to blame ourselves for the things we didn't do or say."

TALKING ABOUT THE FUNERAL

You should strongly encourage your teen to attend the funeral. The funeral service can be a positive learning experience that helps teens share their grief and accept the reality of death.

If your teen has never attended a wake or funeral, it's important to take some time to prepare her for what she'll see and experience, adjusting your information to fit the particular family customs and religious traditions of the deceased. If the deceased is having a wake at a funeral home, for example, describe the setting. Explain that the deceased will be in an open coffin for final viewing and good-byes, but assure your child that she doesn't have to go up close to the body if she chooses not to. Even if you don't personally know the deceased, offer to go along too. Teenagers won't admit it, but they may need your support.

If your teen has already attended a wake or funeral, she knows the details of what she'll see but may still have a lot of questions:

Teen question: "If the body isn't buried right away, doesn't it start to rot?"

Your answer: "When a body isn't buried immediately after death (often because the family wants to keep it for the wake), it is embalmed by a mortician. This is a process that injects certain chemicals into the body to preserve it for a while longer."

Teen question: "How is a body cremated?"
Your answer: "During cremation, the body is not burned with fire, as many people think. It is exposed to an intense heat that reduces it to ashes. These ashes are then collected and placed in an urn. The family may choose to bury the urn, or keep it, or bring it to a place, like the ocean or the mountains, and scatter the ashes out into the world."

Teen question: "Why do people socialize and laugh at the wake?"
Your answer: "People come to a wake to give emotional support to each other at this time of loss. They do this in a variety of ways. Some show their feelings by crying. Others sit in silence. Some pray. And others share stories about the deceased, especially remembering the good times. Others support each other by having social conversations that just for a few moments distract them from their feelings of grief. You should relax at a wake and let your own feelings tell you what's the best way for you to act."

GETTING PROFESSIONAL HELP

Some teens have an exceptionally hard time dealing with the death of a loved one. They get stuck in the grieving process and can't seem to find the other side. If your teen is overwhelmed by grief and is unable to function normally after six months, you should definitely seek mental health intervention. Counseling is available through a variety of community resources, such as school counselors; school psychologists; mental health centers; children and youth services; and psychiatrists, psychologists, and counselors in private practice.

FOR FURTHER READING

Kübler-Ross, Elisabeth. *Death: The Final Stage of Growth*. New York: Simon & Schuster, 1986.

Menten, Ted. *After Goodbye: How to Begin Again After the Death of Someone You Love*. Philadelphia: Running Press, 1994.

Obershaw, Richard. *Cry Until You Laugh: Comforting Guidance for Coping with Grief*. Minneapolis, Minn.: Fairview Press, 1998.

Date Rape

Becky was a sophomore when she began dating Craig, the president of the senior class. Craig was a fun guy to hang around with, and Becky was in heaven when he asked her to the prom. For an entire month Becky planned the evening; she envisioned everything: what they would wear, what they would talk about, what songs they would dance to, what other people would say about the most fabulous couple at the prom. What Becky didn't envision was what would happen on the drive home. All her wonderful memories of the most perfect night of her life were dashed when Craig pulled his car into a secluded area and, after a few minutes of innocent necking, pushed her down on the seat. Becky protested and tried to push him off, but in only seconds, her dress and stockings were ripped, and she was raped.

As most of us do, when teens think of rape they think of the crazed maniac who jumps out of the bushes with a knife or gun and forces a woman to have sex with him. But the truth is, most rapes are not committed by strangers but by men who know their victims, who often have gone out with them previously and are supposedly their friends. This phenomenon is called acquaintance rape or date rape—and it's much more common than most people think. Exact numbers are hard to find because experts estimate that as many as 90 percent of all rapes are never reported. But in a study by the National Center for the Prevention and Control of Rape, 92 percent of adolescent rape victims said they were acquainted with their attackers. This gives us something very important to talk to our teens about.

TALKING TO YOUR SON ABOUT DATE RAPE

The newspapers are full of stories of teenage boys being charged with rape by the girls they were dating, or the girls they met at a party, or the girls they knew casually from school. It seems that as teen sexual activity increases, date rape is becoming more common. Even if you believe your son is not sexually active, it's important to talk to him about this problem. It's never too early for a teen to know how to respect women and what the law says will happen if he doesn't.

Talk About Dangerous "Macho" Attitudes. Ask your son what he thinks about the results of a UCLA study that asked teens about acceptable behavior in dating situations.

Tell him: "A high percentage of the male teens felt that forced sex was acceptable if the woman said yes and then changed her mind (54 percent), if he spent a lot of money on her (39 percent), and if he is so turned on that he thinks he can't stop (36 percent)." *Then ask him:* "What do you think?"

This will open up a discussion in which you can emphatically stress the unacceptability of forced sex. Your son needs to know that rape under any circumstance is a crime of violence and that it is illegal.

Talk About the Bottom Line. "'No' means *no*. Many men who are accused of rape use excuses like, 'She asked for it because she was wearing a sexy dress,' or 'I paid for an expensive dinner, and she was flirting with me,' or 'She was leading me on and then said no at the last second just so I wouldn't think she was easy.' But none of this matters. All that matters is that when a woman says no, there is never a reason to force yourself on her."

Talk About the Role of Alcohol and Drugs. "Many date rapes happen when the man, the woman, or both have had too much alcohol or drugs. The fact that you were intoxicated is not a legal defense of rape. You are responsible for your actions, whether you are sober or not. If a woman has had too much to drink and has passed out or is not in control of herself, having sex with her is still rape."

Talk About Responsibility. "Your desires may be beyond your control, but your actions are within your control. Sexual excitement does not justify forced sex."

Talk About Manliness. "Not having sex or not 'scoring' does not mean you are not a 'real' man. Don't be pressured by any guys at school who push you to do something you know is wrong. A real man respects women and treats them as equals."

Talk About Clear Communication. "It's important to stay in touch with what's really going on. Ask yourself if you are really hearing what she wants, not just what you want. If you have any doubts about what a woman wants, STOP. ASK. CLARIFY."

TALKING TO YOUR DAUGHTER
ABOUT DATE RAPE

Just as certainly as you want your daughter to date and to learn how to socialize with boys, you want her to be safe. That's why it's important to talk about date rape. Experts agree that the more a girl knows about date rape, the more likely it is that she can avoid being put in a situation where it can occur. Thinking and talking about date rape and what she might do if she finds herself in a bad situation can increase her chances of avoiding rape. Your goal in this discussion should be to make her aware without being afraid.

Begin by giving your daughter this generally accepted definition:

"Acquaintance rape is forced, unwanted intercourse with a person you know. It is a violation of your body and your trust. It is an act of violence. It can be with someone you have just met or who you have dated a few times; it can even happen with a steady boyfriend."

Then begin a discussion that will get her to think about her role in avoiding date rape. You should try to touch on each of the following points that are based on information supplied by the Center for Women Policy Studies in Washington, D.C.:

Talk About Mixed Messages. "In all dating situations, be clear about your likes and dislikes. When your date asks you if you want to go to a movie or out to eat, don't waiver and let him decide.

When he asks if you want to double date, say yes when you mean yes and say no when you mean no. If he puts his hand on your knee, and you don't like it—say so, don't ignore it. Always let a date know that you know your own mind and say what you mean."

Talk About Sexual Limits. "It is your body, and no one has the right to force you to do anything you do not want to do. If you do not want someone to touch you or kiss you, for example, you can say, 'Take your hands off me,' or 'Don't touch me,' or 'If you don't respect my wishes right now, I'm leaving.' Stopping sexual activity doesn't mean that anything is wrong with you or that you're not a 'real' woman. It means you know how to speak up for yourself."

Talk About Flirting. "Flirting is fun and natural, but sometimes it can send nonverbal signals of willingness to enter a sexual relationship. Be aware of signals you send with your posture, clothing, tone of voice, gestures, and eye contact. Don't let them say you're ready for sex when you're not."

Talk About Trusting Gut-Level Feelings. "If you feel you are being pressured, you probably are, and you need to respond. If a situation feels bad, or you start to get nervous about the way your date is acting, confront him immediately or leave the situation as quickly as possible."

Talk About Being Independent on Dates. "Let your date know that you are not passive or dependent. Especially on the first few dates, establish your independence by having your own transportation (or at least cab or bus fare) and, if possible, pay your own way or suggest activities."

Talk About the Role of Alcohol and Drugs. "Alcohol and drugs are a significant factor in date rape. Many victims say later that they drank too much or took too many drugs to realize what was going on. Alcohol and drugs make it hard for you and your date to make responsible decisions."

Talk About Falling for Old Lines. "Don't listen when he says, 'You would if you loved me.' If he loves you, he will respect your feelings."

Talk About Vulnerability. "To avoid date rape, you should avoid secluded places where you are in a vulnerable position—especially on the first few dates when you are just getting to know your date. Do not accept invitations into his house or invite him into yours when no one is home. Do not go for walks or drives to out-of-the-way areas. Go where there are other people, where you feel comfortable and safe."

Talk About Friends and Values. "Be careful how you pick your friends. If you hang out with people who are more sexually permissive than you are, you may be perceived as sharing those values."

Talk About What to Do if Things Start to Get out of Hand. "If your date pressures you for sex or starts to force sex, be loud in protesting, leave, go for help. Do not wait for someone else to rescue you or for things to get better. If it feels uncomfortable, leave quickly."

Talk About What to Do if Raped. "Rape is never a woman's fault. No one has the right to use your body in any way that you don't want. If this ever happens to you, I don't want you to hesitate to tell me immediately. This is the kind of thing that a young woman shouldn't have to handle alone. Come to me, tell me, and together we'll deal with it."

Date rape will continue to happen for as long as males believe it's not really rape and as long as females are uncertain how to avoid it. Talk to your teens today.

FOR FURTHER READING

Carter, Christine (ed.). *The Other Side of Silence: Women Tell About Their Experience with Date Rape*. Washington, D.C.: Avocus, 1997.

Warshaw, Robin. *I Never Called It Rape: The Ms. Report on Recognizing, Fighting, and Surviving Date and Acquaintance Rape*. New York: Harper Perennial Library, 1994.

Especially for Teens
Parrot, Andrea. *Coping with Date Rape and Acquaintance Rape*. New York: Rosen Publishing Group, 1995.

Part Two

Forewarnings

Alcohol and **Drinking** and **Driving**

The party was over, and seventeen-year-old Ken decided to walk home rather than take a ride from his friend, who had been drinking. Ken was supposed to be the designated driver that night, but he had had a few too many beers himself, and besides, his friend was acting like a jerk and deserved to find his own way home. As Ken weaved his way along the roads through town, a pickup truck came speeding up from behind and hit him. The driver was a classmate who had been at the same party and who, "like everybody else," drank too much. Ken died instantly, and the driver is now on trial for DWI vehicular homicide. This is a tragedy for both families, one that is repeated over and over again around the world. We all need to talk about it.

I t is your incredibly tough job to convince your kids that alcohol is not an option. It is our view that there is no in-between on this subject. If you allow your teens to drink "only in my house" or "only one drink" or "only on special occasions" or "as long as you promise not to drive," you are giving a green light to, first, something that is illegal and, second, something that they are not yet mature enough to keep within these limits. A study from the Johnson Institute found that when school-age children are allowed to drink alcohol at home, they are not only more likely to use alcohol and other drugs outside the home but also are more likely to develop serious behavioral and health problems related to their use of alcohol and other drugs. Other studies show that fewer than one in three parents of tenth grade students are giving their children a clear "no use" message about alcohol. Don't let that happen in your house. Today is the day to make it clear: "Alcohol is not an option until you're twenty-one. The law backs me up on this one."

WHY YOU SHOULD TALK ABOUT ALCOHOL USE

Teenagers know they should not drink. The law tells them. School programs tell them. Public service ads tell them. But none of these things have the impact that you can have if you talk firmly and directly about your expectations and limits. If your teen hears nothing from you on the subject of alcohol, he will consider your silence permission.

Mothers Against Drunk Driving (MADD) gives us statistics that make it very clear that we have good reason to talk to our teens about alcohol use:

- Alcohol is the number one drug problem among young people.
- Of the twenty million junior high and senior high school students in America, half drink monthly.
- Approximately two-thirds of teenagers who drink report that they can buy their own alcohol.
- Youth who drink alcohol are 7.5 times more likely to use any illicit drug and 50 times more likely to use cocaine than young people who never drink alcohol.

- More than half of the nation's junior high and senior high school students drink alcoholic beverages, and many binge drink to relieve stress and boredom.
- Poor grades are correlated with increased use of alcohol. Alcohol is implicated in more than 40 percent of all academic problems and 28 percent of all dropouts.
- Approximately 240,000 to 360,000 of the nation's 12 million undergraduates will ultimately die from alcohol-related causes—more than the number that will get M.A.'s and Ph.D.'s combined.

Aside from these tragic reasons not to drink, there are many others that directly affect your teen's daily life. When your teens say, "Why not?" tell them: "Alcohol interferes with schoolwork, job performance, athletic ability, social skills, personal relationships, sleep, health and weight management, and energy to do other things in life. It's just not worth such a high price."

TEACH RESPONSIBLE
ALCOHOL USE THROUGH EXAMPLE

If you drink, you will undoubtedly hear, "If drinking is so bad, why do you drink?" Don't respond in anger or with a curt "because the law says I can." This is a good opportunity to sit down and talk about alcohol. Your teen opened the door; don't hesitate to follow into a discussion.

Of course it's true that because adult drinking is not illegal, it is automatically in a whole different category than teen drinking. But talk about *why* the law says you must be twenty-one to drink. Explain that teens don't yet know how to control the impulse to binge drink. They don't have the experience to drink socially without getting drunk. They are more likely to engage in risky acts (such as sex and taking drugs) when drunk. They do not yet have the maturity to use alcohol without abusing it.

This kind of discussion will have an impact only if your own drinking habits are an example of responsible drinking. Get your own drinking habits in line before you use yourself as an example, then you can point out that you don't drink to get drunk, that you drink in moderation, that you drink slowly and never on an empty stomach, that you never drink when you are going to drive. Ask your teen to compare this way of drinking to the way teens drink.

"The difference between responsible use and irresponsible abuse of alcohol is the reason teens are not allowed to drink."

HOW TO TALK ABOUT ALCOHOL USE AND ABUSE

When giving your teen the facts and pointing out the real-life consequences of underage drinking, keep these communication tips in mind:

- Let your actions speak for you. Let your kids hear you say, "No, thanks, I'm driving" when offered that extra drink. Let them see that you don't let anyone who is intoxicated drive away from a family party.
- Be open in expressing your beliefs, values, and feelings. Encourage the same from your teenagers. Let your children know that drunkenness is not accepted by your family.

- Be calm. Remember that you're sharing ideas and information about underage drinking. Don't put your teenager on the witness stand or demand a confession.
- Be a good listener. Let your teenager know that you want to hear what he has to say and learn what he knows about alcohol use and abuse. Listen, even when you may not agree.
- Keep the discussion focused. Your goal is to talk only about the problem of underage drinking—not anything else.
- Remember that a single, one-shot discussion will not do the job. Reinforce your teen's learning with reminders, ongoing discussions, and attention to news stories.
- Praise the good. When your teen has acted responsibly in a difficult situation, show your approval.
- Encourage your teen to stay away from alcohol. Assure her that there are many people, young and old, who do not drink at all. This is the healthiest choice for her body and mind.

As in all discussions with teens, you should not do all the talking—but don't be surprised if your teen has nothing to say. To get her to open up, talk about the general issue of alcohol use rather than her personal use. Talk about stories in the news about teens and drinking, ask her opinions before you give your own, and treat her beliefs with respect even when they are different from yours. Ask:

"Some people think the drinking age should be lowered to eighteen. What do you think?"
"Studies show that an awful lot of teenagers are binge drinking on weekends. Do you see that trend in your school?"
"Some people think that teens who drive drunk should lose their driver's license until they're twenty-one. Do you think that would stop teens from driving drunk?"

WHY YOU SHOULD TALK ABOUT
DRINKING AND DRIVING

Take a look at these statistics:

- Traffic accidents are the greatest single cause of death for people ages six to twenty-eight. Almost half are alcohol related.
- The leading cause of death for fifteen- to twenty-four-year-olds is drunk and drugged driving.
- Eight young people a day die in alcohol-related crashes.

These numbers are enough to tempt any parent to hide the car keys. But, unfortunately, they apparently don't do much to convince teens not to drink and drive—or not to get in a car with a drunk driver. (More than half of the people killed by teen drivers are passengers in their cars.) So you'll need more than gruesome statistics or even pictures of mangled bodies (like the ones your teen will see in her driver education classes) to convince your teen that drinking and driving don't mix. What you'll need is a constant, ongoing discussion about the dangers of drunk driving.

TALK ABOUT THE REALITY
OF TEEN DRINKING AND DRIVING

Long before your teen brings home his driver's permit, the subject of drunk driving should be on the table. Using everyday news events, point out to your young teens how alcohol affects the mind and body. Discuss the dangers of trying to drive while mentally and physically impaired. Show your children newspaper stories about DWI car accidents and legal trials. Let them see, early on, that there are long-term consequences for many people when one person decides to drink and drive.

Pointing to a news story, you can give your opinions without lecturing. You might say:

"Look at this story about a horrible car crash on Route 72. It says here that the drunken driver has two broken legs, and his passenger needed more than two hundred stitches to close up the cuts on her face. What a shame. I'll bet they don't think those drinks were so much fun now. That poor young driver won't be able to walk without a cast or crutches for months, and the girl's face will be scarred forever. Too bad they didn't know that you can't drink and drive."

That's it. You don't need to lecture; you don't have to condemn. You can simply show your teen a real-life example of the consequences of drinking and driving. This kind of news story is a particularly good example because the driver didn't die. Believe it or not, teens don't fear death as much as they do injury and disfigurement. Saying, "You could kill yourself" doesn't carry the impact of saying, "You could break your arms or lose your eyesight." Maybe the image of having his legs in a cast and missing baseball season will prompt your son to refuse a ride home from a drunken friend. Or your daughter may be horrified enough at the thought of a scarred face to do the same. With this approach, you're not lecturing your young teen about what to do or not to do. ("Don't you ever get in the car with someone who has been drinking.") Instead, you're giving him information and images to decide for himself that he doesn't want any part of drinking and driving.

Whether or not your teen drinks is not always the issue. As long as there are teenagers, there are going to be parties where alcohol is available and where your teen will be in a position to make decisions about getting in a car with a driver who has been drinking. Your teen needs to know how much alcohol is too much and why the impaired driver may look, act, and sound perfectly sober. To impress these facts on your teen, you'll need to know the details of alcohol absorption in the body. If you want your teen to trust and believe you, you've got to have your facts straight.

A general rule of thumb says you should wait one hour per drink before driving to allow the return of the muscular coordination, concentration, and good judgment necessary for safe driving. It has been found that two or three drinks in an hour can bring the average individual's blood alcohol level to .05 percent. Studies have shown that a driver whose blood alcohol level is just .04 percent is seven times more likely to have an accident than a nondrinker. So judgment and reaction time are impaired before a person drinks enough to become legally drunk. When a person's blood alcohol concentration reaches .10 percent (about four drinks in an hour if the person weighs 160 pounds), voluntary actions become clumsy. Someone in this condition is judged to be legally drunk in all fifty states.

Your teen needs to know that all the fresh air, coffee, and cold showers in the world will not change his blood alcohol level. Alcohol is absorbed quickly into the body through the bloodstream, but it takes a long time to leave it. Alcohol passes directly through the walls of the stomach and the small intestine without being digested; it is distributed to body tissue and cells and carried quickly to the brain. The absorption process is slowed down a little if food is in the stomach, but changes in behavior start as soon as the alcohol reaches the brain.

The body consumes about a half-ounce of alcohol per hour. This amount is equivalent to twelve ounces of beer, a half-ounce shot of whiskey or vodka, or a five-ounce glass of table wine. Nothing can hurry up the body's consumption of alcohol; once it's in the body, only time will reduce its concentration in the blood.

So how many drinks does it take to get drunk? The level of blood alcohol concentration (BAC) determines the degree of intoxication. But you can't set a definitive number of drinks that cause drunkenness because the BAC level depends on several factors: body weight, amount of alcohol consumed, amount of food in the stomach, and drinking time. Your teen needs to know that *zero* is the number of drinks she can have before driving. For young, inexperienced drivers, there is no safe drinking and driving zone.

TALK ABOUT ALTERNATIVES TO DRINKING AND DRIVING

Talking about drinking and driving is a good start, but it's not enough. Your teens need to know what to do when they're in a circumstance where there is drinking and driving going on. On prom night, on New Year's Eve, and even after weekend dances, there is going to be drinking. Help your teen plan ahead what he'll do when this happens. Ask your teen what she thinks she'll do if she needs a ride home but the driver has been drinking. Listen to her ideas, discuss them, and help her choose ones she's most comfortable with. If she can't decide what to do, throw out some of the following ideas and see which ones your teen goes for:

- If she has her license, she can offer to drive the car for a drunken friend.
- She can call home at any hour to ask you for a ride.

- If the party is at the home of a friend, she can stay overnight.
- She can use the buddy system (much like the ones used for swimming and gymnastics). A buddy is a person who agrees to stay sober too; your child and her buddy agree to take responsibility for each other's safety.

When you have agreed on a plan, sign a formal contract in which both of you agree to take certain actions when she is in a situation involving drinking and cars. Teens and adults are more likely to keep a promise if they actually sign their name to a formal document that spells out specifically what that promise is, as opposed to just agreeing to it verbally. The agreement for the second idea above might read like this:

Teen: I agree to call you for transportation if I am ever in a situation where I have had too much to drink or if a friend who drove has had too much to drink.

Parent: I agree to come and get you at any hour, any time, any place, no questions asked and no argument. If I am not available, I will pay for a taxi to bring you home.

Signed:

Teen _____ Parent_____

Talking to teens about drinking and driving works. Since the institution of school programs and national initiatives to stop teens from driving drunk (from 1985 to 1995), the proportion of drivers sixteen to twenty years of age who were involved in fatal crashes (and were intoxicated) dropped 47 percent! You can make a difference and save young lives if you speak up and talk to your teens.

TALKING TO TEENS WHO ABUSE ALCOHOL

Many parents are unaware that their teens are abusing alcohol. Many choose to be unaware by ignoring the signs and symptoms. This pushes the problem aside and gives teens silent permission to continue. To protect your teens you must pay attention to their lives, be involved, know what they are doing, and stay alert for any of these signs of alcohol abuse offered by the Substance Abuse and Mental Health Services Administration. Your teen may be abusing alcohol if he or she

Is unable to control drinking
Uses alcohol to escape problems
Has changed from a usually reserved character into the "life of the party"
Has undergone a change in personality
Has a high tolerance for alcohol
Experiences blackouts
Has problems at school as a result of drinking

In addition to these signs, don't ignore the obvious: slurred speech, the smell of alcohol, uncoordinated movements, glazed eyes, and vehement denial of alcohol use.

If you worry that your teen may be abusing alcohol, don't wait for the phase to pass. This is a situation that needs to be addressed immediately:

- Confront your teen with your suspicions. Tell him you're worried.
- Give your reasons for having these suspicions.
- Speak in a caring, understanding tone of voice; do not accuse, attack, or threaten.
- Be prepared for denial and anger. Your teen may say there is nothing wrong and get angry at you for bringing up the subject. Many people with alcohol problems react this way.
- Find out where help is available—and get it. There are numerous national, state, and local organizations, treatment centers, and referral centers, and there are hotlines throughout the country. Look in your phone book under community drug hotlines, community treatment services, city and local health departments, Alcoholics Anonymous, Al-Anon or Alateen, or hospitals.

Many teens experiment with alcohol and go on to live long, productive lives. But teens who regularly abuse alcohol are on a path to self-destruction and need your help. Don't fail them by looking the other way.

RESOURCES

Al-Anon/Alateen Family Group Headquarters
P.O. Box 862
Midtown Station
New York, NY 10018
(800) 344-2666

Mothers Against Drunk Driving
669 Airport Freeway, Suite 310
Hurst, TX 76053
(817) 268-6233
Web site: http://www.madd.org

National Clearinghouse for Alcohol and Drug Information
P.O. Box 2345
Rockville, MD 20852
(301) 468-2600
Web site: http://www.health.org

Call to receive free informational pamphlets. Recommended:
"Tips for Teens About Alcohol."

FOR FURTHER READING

Johnston, Jerry. *It's Killing Our Kids*. Irving, Tex.: Word Publishing, 1991.

Vogler, Roger, and Wayne Bortz. *Teenagers and Alcohol: When Saying No Isn't Enough*. Seattle: Charles Press, 1992.

Especially for Teens
Debenedette, Valerie. *Alcohol and You*. Springfield, N.J.: Enslow, 1996.

Shellenberger, Susie, and Greg Johnson. *Cars, Curfews, Parties, and Parents*. Minneapolis, Minn.: Bethany House, 1995.

Dangers on the World Wide Web

At Joe's fiftieth birthday party, the adults gathered in the kitchen, and the kids ran downstairs to the family room. For hours everyone talked, laughed, and partied—it was great night. On the way home, Ted asked his fourteen-year-old daughter what all the laughing was about downstairs. "Oh, we had the best time!" Katie said. "Their computer is on-line, and we were in these chat rooms talking to people all over the country. There was this one guy who's in the Army, and he kept writing messages to me. He wants to meet me!" she gushed. "Dad, can't we get the Internet too?" Ted's heart sank. It was an awful feeling to think that while he was having a good time with friends upstairs, his daughter was being preyed upon by adult strangers downstairs—and she had no idea how dangerous the game could become.

"It's late right now," Ted said, "but in the morning we'll talk about using the Internet. There's a few things you need to know about what you can and cannot do when you're on-line."

"Oh, Dad," Katie groaned as she crossed her arms and sank deeper into the backseat.

Times sure have changed. When our children were young, strangers, child molesters, and racists lived on the streets, where we could control their influence on our children. But now, our teens are inviting these predators into our homes for a chat. What was once unthinkable is now an everyday reality.

THE GOOD AND THE BAD

The Internet is not a bad thing. It opens the door to a vast collection of very positive informational and entertaining material. To be able to sit at home and view the Louvre's art collection, take a trip to the Smithsonian, or access research from top academic institutions across the country is an impressive feat of modern technology. The Internet as a homework helper has unlimited positive potential. But the Net also has its dark side that becomes more and more difficult to control as your kids enter their teen years. Adult and child pornography, boy-lovers' support groups, pedophiles in kids' chat rooms, foul-mouthed creeps, deceptive advertising, market research ploys, and American Nazi and Klan propaganda are all thrown into the cyberspace mix. Insidiously, these evil intruders creep into your home while you're in the next room, pleased that your teen is making good use of the computer instead of watching mindless TV.

Some parents are unconcerned about teen use of the Internet, believing that it's just another way for kids to explore the facts of life. But viewing smut on the Internet is more serious than slipping into the adult section of the library and taking a peek into forbidden territory. The Internet is interactive. It's more like having adult neighbors who lure our kids into their homes to wine and dine them and then abuse their innocence. This deserves our attention.

Some parents address the problem by keeping the Internet out of their homes completely. But this isn't an entirely satisfactory solution. The Internet is a part of our world that we can't keep hidden from our teens. It's in their schools, in the libraries, and in their friends' homes. The Internet, with its good and bad, is here. The challenge is to limit our teens' access to adult sites and then to talk to them so they know where the limits are, why there are limits, and what to do to protect themselves from exceeding those limits.

USING BLOCKING DEVICES

There are a number of ways you can block access on your computer to certain kinds of subjects. Some major Internet access providers, such as America Online and CompuServe, allow parents to customize restrictions by blocking access to sites whose names include words you want to avoid, such as *sex* or *Satan*. You can also block participation in on-line chat rooms and allow a person to exchange e-mail only with preapproved addresses. You can also limit site access only to sites approved by two Internet organizations—the Recreational Software Advisory Council and SafeSurf. There is also "baby-sitting" software that you can install to act as a high-tech chaperone. Each product steers users clear of its own list of bad places and wards off other risks, such as foul language or the ability to disclose a name, address, phone number, or credit card number.

These so-called safety devices are very popular, but they have major drawbacks for teens:

New sites pop up every day that are not included on the programmed list of blocked sites.

Computer-experienced teens will find ways around even the
    best filters.
Yours is not the only computer in town with access to the
    Internet. Your teen has access at school, in the library, and
    at friends' homes.

These filters are better than nothing, especially if your teen is
home alone after school. But the real issue is what you tell your teen
about the reason for the blocking devices. Why can't he search for
"sex" just for the fun of seeing what happens? Why can't she give
out her address and phone number? Even if you could find an infal-
lible way to keep the smut off your home computer, you'd still need
to talk to your teen about the fact that it's out there, the reasons why
you don't want it in your home, and the reasons why he or she
shouldn't visit those sites at any time on any computer.

TALKING AGAIN ABOUT STRANGER SAFETY

Ask your kids, "Remember when we used to talk about stranger
safety? Remember when we used to practice what to do if a stranger
asked you to go with him? Well, it's time to update our lessons on
how to deal with strangers."

At this point your teens will roll their eyes and say, "Oh come
on. Leave me alone." But when you point out that you're talking
about strangers on the Internet, they may be curious.

If you have filters on your computer (or plan to install them),
tell your teen that you want him to understand why these are
necessary.

"There are certain people," you might begin, "who are not welcomed in my home. I would not open my door to a stranger carrying a portfolio of pornographic pictures that he wanted to show to my children. How ridiculous to even think that I would let that happen. I wouldn't sit down for a chat with a person who said she wanted to teach my children about prejudice and hatred; you'd think I was crazy if I did. I would be a terrible parent if I didn't warn you not to open the door to known child molesters and perverts. Well, I also won't welcome these same people into my home through the Internet. It's no different than having them come sit in my living room. Blocking their access is not blocking your ability to use the Internet for hundreds of entertaining and educational uses; it's protecting you from the intrusion of strangers who are not welcome here."

USING TEACHABLE MOMENTS ON THE INTERNET

Whether you have filters or not, the Internet gives you a valuable and objective medium with which to broach sensitive subjects with your teens. When you explain why they are not allowed to download pornographic pictures, you can explain the reasons why pornography is a bad thing (see "Pornography" for the details). When you limit their access to sites authored by American Nazis or the Ku Klux Klan, this is a good time to discuss prejudice and the pain it has brought to humankind (see "Prejudice"). When you ban sexually explicit material, offer your feelings about the responsibility and privacy issues that go along with sexuality (see "Sex, Contraception, and Pregnancy"). And forbidding on-line exploration of satanism gives you the perfect opening to explain why this practice is unacceptable to you (see "Cults").

Take the dark side of the Internet and turn it to your advantage. Let it be the vehicle you use to talk to your teens about really important things.

TAKE A FIRM STAND

Even when your teens know why certain sites are off-limits, expect that they will still be curious. Patrolling their use of the Internet is no different than keeping an eye on any other of their leisure-time activities. Let them know where you stand and what you intend to do about it.

Tell your teens that to keep track of their surfing habits, you're going to put the computer in a central location through which family traffic routinely passes: the family room, the den, the living room, or even the kitchen. If your teen has the computer in his or her bedroom and you can't move it, make it known that you plan to visit often.

There's no need to hide the fact that you want to keep track of your teens' Internet use. Tell them, "Just as I wouldn't let you go unsupervised into a major city without any idea of your plans, I won't let you go off into the Internet without any supervision or agreement on your destination. This is part of being a good parent."

After your talk, take one last step toward peace of mind by making sure your teens agree to follow these three "Never" rules recommended by law enforcement officials:

1. Never give out identifying information, such as an address, school name, telephone number, picture, or password to anyone on-line.

2. Never arrange a face-to-face meeting without parental permission. (Make any agreed-on meetings in public or in your own home when you are present.)
3. Never respond to messages that are belligerent or sexually suggestive. (If your teen receives these kinds of messages, make sure she knows how to make a copy of the message to forward to your service provider.)

The World Wide Web is at our children's fingertips, and they will find whatever information they are determined to find. But don't let that influence your decision to talk about what's out there and to explain why some sites are off-limits. Your kids may groan, but that doesn't mean they're not listening. Survey after survey of teens reveals that most of them want to be protected by their parents; they want to know their parents care enough about them to make the hard decisions. It's only in disgust that a teen will say, "My parents don't care what I do."

FOR FURTHER READING

Kehoe, Brendan, and Victoria Anne Mixon. *Children and the Internet: A Zen Guide for Parents and Educators*. Upper Saddle River, N.J.: Prentice Hall, 1997.

Drug Abuse

"Look what I have."

"Where'd you get a joint?"

"Never mind where I got it—let's smoke it."

"I don't know. Won't we get in trouble?"

"Don't be such a baby. How can we get in trouble if nobody knows? Come on."

"But what about cheerleading practice?"

"We'll make it on time; I have my dad's car. And besides, pot loosens you up and makes it easier to do splits and stuff. It'll be great."

"Well all right. If you're sure it's OK."

This dialogue between two fourteen-year-olds is fictional, but you'd better believe that thousands of conversations just like it occur in thousands of homes and schools all over this country. In fact, the majority of our children will be engaged in this kind of discussion at one time or another. Before that happens, it's time to talk.

THINK ABOUT YOUR OWN DRUG USE

Before you make the effort to talk to your teens about drugs, take some time to think about your own use of drugs. We all use them. We take them to ease physical and emotional pains. We take them when we have a cold, when we have a headache, when we're tired, when we need to relax. Drugs are so much a part of our culture that we don't even think of them as drugs. But it's this casual use of legal drugs that gives our teens the impression that drug use is no big deal. They are bombarded with media messages that drugs are good, therapeutic, and necessary. Drugs provide fast solutions to problems. It's in this environment that your kids will be listening to your antidrug messages. You can give these messages more impact if you first monitor your own drug use and the way you talk about the miracles of modern-day medicines.

Explain that some drugs are legal and that using them sensibly is not necessarily bad. At the same time, use prescription and over-the-counter drugs with caution and explanation. Try to avoid taking any medications in front of your teens, and when you must, talk about the reason. You might say, "I'm taking this cold medicine because a drug like this can be helpful if I don't take too much or use it too often." Let your kids know that drugs are taken only for positive medicinal purposes. Avoid comments like, "Boy, do I need a cigarette." "What a day! Where are the aspirins?" "When I get home, I'm going to have a stiff drink." Remarks like these convey the idea that it's acceptable to use drugs to quickly change one's mood.

WHY TALK ABOUT DRUGS

According to a survey by the National Institute on Drug Abuse (NIDA), more than 1.6 million children ages twelve to seventeen

use illicit drugs. The NIDA survey also found that the average age
at which a child initially uses marijuana is twelve. Statistics also tell
us that drug abuse is not something that happens only to other people's kids or only in big cities. We all know stories about good kids
from good families whose lives were ruined by drugs.

So how do we keep our teens safe and healthy? Research studies repeatedly show that a child's family has a strong influence over
his or her likelihood of abusing drugs. Parental love, guidance, and
support help children develop self-esteem, self-confidence, personal
values, and goals—all of which contribute to the making of drug-
free kids. This chapter will look at a small piece of this big family
picture: the role of family communication in preventing drug abuse.

DRAW THE LINE ON DRUGS

Make sure your teens know where you stand on drug use. Remember, silence is often interpreted by hopeful teens as permission. Say:

"I have no doubt that someone will offer you drugs. You'll be encour-
aged to drink, smoke dope, or even to take cocaine or pills. You
know I feel strongly that illegal drugs are very dangerous. They're
not good for your body or your mind, and they can kill you. I'm not
going to give you a lecture about how bad they are for you because
you've probably already learned a lot about them in school. But I
want you to think about this: You—plain and simple—don't need
them. You have too much going for you. Drugs don't really help anything. They don't solve problems. They won't make you popular.
They won't help you grow up. And they surely won't help you build
a strong body and mind. In fact, just the opposite can happen. I
want you to know that I will not condone illicit drug use by anyone
in this family, and I trust you to make the right decision."

This kind of statement lets your teens know that you understand that drugs are readily available and that there is peer pressure to give them a try. It also tells them that you know they know about the dangers of drugs and that you have faith in their ability to make responsible and smart decisions.

When you draw the line on drug use, make it firmly against *all* harmful drugs. When parents get a call from the school informing them that their teens have been caught with drugs, many are relieved to find it is "only" alcohol, cigarettes, or marijuana. Experts don't share this sense of relief. They know that these "gateway" drugs are the ones that aim kids toward more sustained and serious addictions. Almost five million teenagers have drinking problems, and alcohol- and drug-related accidents are the leading cause of death for teenagers. (See "Alcohol and Drinking and Driving" for more information.) Smoking is responsible for close to 450,000 deaths each year, and young cigarette smokers are one hundred times more likely than nonsmokers to smoke pot and become addicted to other illicit substances such as heroin and cocaine.

STUDY THE FACTS
AND SHARE WHAT YOU FIND

To discuss drug use and abuse with your teens, you need the most up-to-date facts. You can't convince them that you know what you're talking about if you use old, outdated terms or information. So now is the time to study up on illicit drugs, learn the facts, and keep up on the lingo. We can't begin to detail all these facts here, but the resources listed at the end of this chapter will help you easily find the information you need.

As you begin your discussions about drug abuse, you don't have to hide the fact that you don't know everything. When you obtain material you want to study, share it with your child; explore it together; state clearly that because you love your child very much, you want to learn all about the drug abuse problem that affects so many young people.

You might look up from your reading and ask questions like these:

"Did you know that sniffing glue, nail polish remover, or correction fluid can cause irreversible brain damage?"

"I just read that one in five teenagers smokes cigarettes. When you look around a classroom filled with twenty students, do you think at least four are smokers?"

"Why do kids smoke when we know that nicotine is addictive and smoking is a known killer?"

"Do you think it's true that nearly 40 percent of teenagers try marijuana before they graduate high school?"

"It says here that some children are starting to use crack in elementary school. Why do you think they do that?"

"It's illegal to smoke marijuana. Do you know why?"

As you search for the facts, find out if drug education is a part of your school's curriculum. If it is, ask your teen's teachers to tell you when the topic will be discussed and exactly what is in the lesson. Use this information to further explore the subject at home. Ask your kids, "What did you learn in class today about drugs?" Then take some time to combine this information with your family's values, beliefs, and feelings.

TALK ABOUT DRUG ABUSE

Don't assume that because your kids don't talk or ask questions about drug use or abuse, they're not interested and it doesn't affect their lives. You will probably have to jump-start the conversations on this subject. And remember that talking about drugs should not be a one-shot deal. You should look for opportunities to talk fairly regularly about the negative effects of drug use.

Talk About the Immediate Effects of Drugs. It's best to avoid focusing on the long-term future effects of drug abuse. Teens have only a limited interest in the future. Instead, talk about now: the potential for loss of power and control over themselves, the interference with goals they want to achieve, the effects on their moods, and the possibility of accidental death. You can use news stories of lives ruined by drug use. You can use stories of athletes and drug arrests. You can use information about local cases of drug arrests. Show them that using drugs affects the quality of their life right now.

Let's say, for example, that a local teen is arrested for having a bag of marijuana in her car. You might say:

"What a shame. I remember when Sue was such a good basketball player and a good student too. But getting into drugs is probably the reason she's lost interest in sports and school. I've heard that she's been hanging out with a lot of kids who do drugs. Do you think that has anything to do with the trouble she's having in school?"

Talk About Individual Reactions to Drugs. Your teens probably knows teens who use drugs and appear to be perfectly healthy. So talk about the unpredictability of drugs bought on the street and the idiosyncratic and dangerous reactions of each individual to drugs.

The unexpected drug deaths of young, famous personalities are perfect examples of this danger. You might say:

"What a shame that so-and-so died over the weekend of a drug overdose. I'm sure he had taken drugs before and had no idea that this hit would be his last. Why do you think they killed him this time?"

Talk About Drug Advertising. Information about the good and bad sides of drugs can be conveyed through advertisements for medications, alcohol, and cigarettes. TV, radio, and print ads promise that life's physical and social problems can be instantly cured with a pill, a cigarette, or a drink. Kids see adults buying remedies for everything that ails them—this message that chemical substances can cure all our ills and promote beauty, success, and fun is a dangerous one. It doesn't show the physical consequences—hangovers, vomiting, and addiction—or the social realities of daily stress and personal beauty. When your children are exposed to these ads, ask them questions like these:

"Do you think it's the cigarette that really makes that woman feel happy?"
"What will happen if that man quickly drinks that whole bottle of liquor?"
"Can you think of something besides that sleeping pill that might help the lady fall asleep?"
"If all those spicy foods make that man's stomach hurt, how could he stop having stomachaches without taking that medicine?"

Talk About the News. You can use the media to give your children a balanced picture of drug use in America. Scan the daily papers and circle articles related to drug use. Some will show the devastating effects of alcohol-related car accidents, drug-war murders, and lung cancer deaths. Others will highlight lifesaving medicines and breakthrough medical discoveries. These stores give you opportunities to teach your children the difference between responsible use and life-threatening abuse.

TALK ABOUT SAYING NO

Saying no to drugs is a skill of self-assertion. Teens who can resist peer pressure gain confidence and develop a positive self-image that helps them say no again and again in the future. But the effectiveness of this strategy is weak unless your children have opportunities to think about *how* they will say no. The following "Say No Tips" are adapted from a list suggested by drug prevention experts of the National Institute on Drug Abuse. Talk to your kids about these six ways to say no. Let them pick out the ones that feel most comfortable to use and then role-play situations in which these responses might be useful.

1. *Give a reason.* If kids know the facts, they won't be fooled if someone tells them that it feels good to be stoned. Tell your kids they can say something like, "No, I know it's bad for me. I feel fine right now."
2. *Have something else to do.* Kids should know they can say no and then leave. Help them practice saying, "No, thanks. I'm going to get something to eat."
3. *Make it simple.* Tell your kids that they don't have to explain why they don't want to use drugs if they don't want to. They

can just say no. If that doesn't work, help them practice saying no again, or even stronger: no way.

4. *Avoid the situation.* If your kids see or know of places where
people often use drugs, impress on them the importance of
staying away from those places. If they hear that people will
be using drugs at a party, remind them of your family rule
against partying with drugs and let them use you as an excuse.
Encourage them to say, "My parents won't let me go."

5. *Change the subject.* Help your teens be prepared with a statement
that will quickly change the subject. Tell them, for example,
that if someone says, "Let's try some pot," they can say, "No, I
was on my way to the store. Do you want to come along?"

6. *Hang out with friends who don't use drugs.* This is an ideal way
to avoid peer pressure. Stay involved with your kids, meet their
friends, and encourage activities that put them in contact with
other kids who are involved in school, community, or religious
activities. In addition, talk to your teens about the qualities of
true friendship. Tell them, "Real friends won't get mad when
you say no. Real friends won't ridicule or threaten you for
standing up for what you believe in."

BE HONEST ABOUT YOUR OWN EXPERIENCES

When you open the door to discussions about drugs, don't be surprised if your kids want to know if you ever smoked pot, used other
illegal drugs, or engaged in underage drinking. Considering that the
media have broadcast even President Clinton's experimental marijuana use, the casual drug use of the sixties and seventies is bound
to come back to haunt many parents.

If you did smoke pot, pop pills, shoot heroin, use any other illegal drugs or abuse alcohol, truthfulness with clarification is the best way to respond to your kids questions. If you lie or are evasive, you'll lose credibility in your kids' eyes when they probe relatives and old friends and find out the real story. Tell them:

"Yes, I made a mistake, and if I had to do it over again I wouldn't."

Point out your personal knowledge of the adverse effects and dangers of your use:

"I remember driving while I was high and putting myself and everyone in the car in great danger. It was a stupid and dangerous thing to do."

Without implying justification, explain the social climate of the times:

"Drugs were a part of the youth culture; they were often as freely available at parties as potato chips are today. Also, all the facts about the dangers and long-term effects of drug use weren't in yet."

Caution your kids that the dangers of drug use then were less than today. Barbara McCrady, professor of psychology and the clinical director for the Center of Alcohol Studies at Rutgers University, has found that "the marijuana around now is much, much stronger. Drug clinics today are even reporting withdrawal symptoms from it, which was unheard of years ago. The potential for danger from drugs that were once pretty innocuous is far higher."

TALKING TO KIDS WHO USE DRUGS

Communication is the key to the prevention of drug use and abuse. But if you find that your teen is involved with drug use, open, honest communication is still your best tool. If your teen is arrested for drug possession, or if you find drugs in his or her room, or if he or she comes home obviously drunk or stoned, you can't assume this is a one-time mistake that "will never happen again," as your teen will promise. You need to address the situation directly and seriously.

Think Before You Talk
Think first about what you should *not* do:

- Don't try to reason with your teen or argue when he or she is high.
- Don't try to talk when you are too angry or hurt to be coherent and reasonable.
- Don't verbally attack your child; he or she needs your help.
- Don't become hysterical and exaggerate the dangers of drugs; you will seem ridiculous and out of touch.
- Don't label your teen a drug addict. This is an overreaction.
- Don't ignore the problem as "typical teen experimentation." This gives teens permission to continue "experimenting" on the grounds that "you don't care what I do."

Be slow to rescue a teen from the penalties associated with drug misuse. A few hours at police headquarters or having to pay the lawyer's fee for a charge of possession teach powerful lessons.

Be Firm

Take a firm stand against drug use and let your teen know that you are upset about his experimentation. Make it clear (again) that your family has a "no drug" rule. The National Institute on Drug Abuse (NIDA) advises parents to back up this rule with a clear and consistent set of behavioral rules that they are willing to enforce. During the period when your child's natural impulses are to experiment and to test the boundaries, it is vitally important that you give her strong, fair limits by which to define herself. In countless interviews with drug-troubled older teenagers, one hears complaints about parents being hypocritical, inconsistent, permissive, selfish, or aloof, but almost never any complaints about strictness, rules, curfews, chaperoning, or involvement. When making and enforcing rules to guide your children through this difficult time, remember: *Don't be afraid to be a strong parent.* State firmly:

> *The rule:* You cannot use illegal drugs.
> *The consequence:* If you do, you will [insert a punishment that
>   you think is appropriate, such as being grounded for one
>   month or losing all electronic privileges (TV, computer,
>   video, phone, and so on)].
> *The future plan:* Make sure your teen knows that if he does
>   not learn from the punishment, he will begin professional
>   therapy for drug counseling and rehabilitation (see details
>   below).

Be Smart

Tell your teen why you are upset by her drug use and insist that both of you educate yourselves better about illegal drugs and their effects. Talk about the facts—not the fears. Talk about the harmful consequences of using drugs of unknown ingredients, about lethal combinations such as alcohol and barbiturates, about the unexpected effects of various dosage levels, about the hazards of drugs with a strong potential for dependence, and about the legal consequences of being caught using them.

Before you talk, have the facts. The resources listed at the end of this chapter will help you know what to say to your teen.

Be Supportive and Involved

If your teen is into drugs, you must begin a family effort to curtail it. Spend more time with your teen. Get to know his friends. Be alert to other problems, such as a breakup, trouble in school, poor choice of friends, low tolerance for frustration, loneliness. If you can zero in on these things that can drive kids to drugs, you can help your teen open up and talk about the problem. He needs to know that you support him and want to help.

Make sure your teen knows that you love her. You do this when you keep the channels of communication open even when you feel hurt and betrayed. You do this when you offer help rather than sarcastic ridicule. You do this when you set firm rules and consequences, enforce them consistently, and at the same time make yourself available to talk and offer support and encouragement.

Seek Professional Help

If your teen's "experimentation" seems to have become a habit, you'll need professional help to stop the drug use. Your teen will not think this is a great idea, so you will probably do this against his will. There are many adolescent counselors who specialize in therapy and rehabilitation, but take some time to find the one whose views are compatible with yours. Some condone a juvenile's "responsible use" of illegal drugs; others advocate drug-free behavior for the teen. You have the right to ask about the counselor's philosophy before making an appointment.

Whether or not your teen is involved with drugs, talking about drug use and abuse is not a one-time thing. It's an ongoing dialogue that will change in depth and content as your children grow—so keep the conversation going. Use teachable moments offered by TV, commercials, MTV, newspapers, and your teens' own life experiences to let them know that you're informed and concerned and always available to talk about this important topic.

RESOURCES

American Council for Drug Education
204 Monroe Street, Suite 110
Rockville, MD 20850
(301) 294-0600

Marijuana Anonymous, World Services
P.O. Box 2912
Van Nuys, CA 91404
(800) 766-6779

Narcotics Anonymous
P.O. Box 9999
Van Nuys, CA 91409
(818) 773-9999

National Clearinghouse for Alcohol and Drug Information
P.O. Box 2345
Rockville, MD 20852
(301) 468-2600

Call to receive free informational pamphlets. We recommend these:

"Marijuana: Facts Parents Need to Know," NIH Pub. No. 95-4036; "Preventing Drug Use Among Children and Adolescents," NIH Pub. No. 97-4212; and "Tips for Teens," a series of pamphlets on smoking, marijuana, crack and cocaine, inhalants, hallucinogens, and steroids.

PRIDE (National Parents' Resource Institute for Drug Education)
50 Hurt Plaza, Suite 210
Atlanta, GA 30303
(404) 577-4500

FOR FURTHER READING

Baron, Jason D. *Kids and Drugs: A Parent's Handbook of Drug Abuse, Prevention and Treatment.* New York: Perigee Books, 1984.

DeStefano, Susan. *Drugs and the Family.* Frederick, Md.: Twenty-First Century Books, 1991.

Treadway, David. *Before It's Too Late: Working with Substance Abuse in the Family.* New York: Norton, 1989.

U.S. Department of Education. *Growing Up Drug Free: A Parent's Guide to Prevention.* Washington, D.C.: U.S. Department of Education, 1990.

West, James W., and Betty Ford. *The Betty Ford Center Book of Answers: Help for Those Struggling with Substance Abuse and for the People Who Love Them.* New York: Pocket Books, 1997.

Especially for Teens
McFarland, Rhoda. *Drugs and Your Parents.* New York: Rosen Publishing Group, 1997.

HIV/AIDS

"I like tongue kissing," Karen confided to her girlfriend. "But I get really worried about getting AIDS from the saliva."

"What if a kid on the other team has HIV," Jerry wondered to himself. "And his sweat got into my body when we banged into each other. I could have HIV right now!"

"I love Tony," thought Adele. "And I'd like to marry him when we graduate. But what if he got infected with HIV when he used to shoot drugs? What if he gives it to me, and I pass it on to our children?"

For teens, life and love just aren't as much fun as they used to be—or should be. It seems there's no such thing as being carefree anymore now that HIV and AIDS are a very real part of growing up. The Centers for Disease Control and Prevention estimate that half of all new HIV infections in the United States are among people under age twenty-five. HIV (the human immunodeficiency virus) isn't something we can close our eyes to and hope with fingers crossed that it won't touch our kids. It's here, it's real, and it's epidemic. Only a clear understanding of what this virus is, how it is transmitted, and how we can stay safe will let our teens live their lives in good health and without undue fear.

Because AIDS (acquired immunodeficiency syndrome) is a reality of our times, almost all junior high and high schools include information about AIDS in their health curriculum. But getting the facts in a classroom doesn't take away all the fears and questions. In addition to their classroom learning, kids need to know that they can talk to you about this sensitive subject without fear of being lectured, ridiculed, or put off. Most kids don't want to raise their hand and ask if they can get HIV when they play a sport. They need to know that they can talk to you about this "intimate" stuff without being embarrassed and without getting the runaround.

WHEN TO TALK

It's not easy to bring up the subject of HIV/AIDS. It's silly to even think about saying, "Oh, by the way, Jason, tonight why don't we sit down and talk about AIDS." It won't work. This is a subject that is best broached in some kind of social context. If you notice that your teen is doing a report on AIDS or reading a chapter on HIV in a textbook, that would be a good time to ask, "What are you learning in school about AIDS?" If you're both watching the news and you hear a report about AIDS, that's an opening for you to comment on the epidemic and get a discussion going about how your teen and his friends feel about the problem. Then you can add, "Do you have any questions about HIV or AIDS?" Most likely your teen will say no, so leave the door open by adding, "If you ever have a question or if there's anything on your mind about HIV or AIDS, I want you to know that you can ask me. If I don't have the information you need, we'll find it together." Just knowing that AIDS isn't a taboo subject in your house is in itself reassuring.

HOW TO TALK

Don't lecture. A discussion about HIV/AIDS should not be a studied and rehearsed presentation. Make it a conversation, an exchange of information and ideas, a give-and-take of feelings and facts. Your discussion of AIDS should also be an ongoing one, not a one-shot deal. Teens are receptive to different information at different times; as they mature, you should keep talking and listening and let them know that you are always open to questions.

WHAT TO SAY

If you happen to live in an area where HIV/AIDS is not part of the school curriculum, then run to your local bookstore and buy (or order) one of the books recommended for teens at the end of this chapter. Read it yourself to gain a basic understanding of the epidemic, then give it to your teen. He or she must have a foundation of knowledge about this deadly epidemic. Once you both are clear on the basics of what HIV is, how it progresses to AIDS, and how it is transmitted, then move on to the section that looks at the often misunderstood aspects of HIV/AIDS.

In most cases, where HIV/AIDS is part of the school curriculum, we don't recommend that you begin talking to your teens about the basics. They know by heart by now that AIDS is an acronym for Acquired Immunodeficiency Syndrome; they know that it is caused by a virus called the human immunodeficiency virus. What they need from you that they might not get at school or from their friends is some clarification about how HIV affects them personally and a place to go when the facts get mixed up.

The following are responses you can give to statements your teen might make that show some confusion or uncertainty about the facts. If your teen doesn't come right out with these kinds of blunders, you can sprinkle the information into the conversations about HIV/AIDS that pop up in response to some school or media mention of the epidemic.

Experts who work with teenagers have found that these are the issues most frequently misunderstood:

Mixing Up the Definitions of HIV and AIDS

Teen comment: "At school they said that you can't tell if someone has AIDS. That's crazy. In all the pictures they keep showing us of people with AIDS I could tell right away—they look really sick."

Your response: "You're right; people with full-blown AIDS are very sick, and they often look it. But in the beginning, people who are infected with the virus that causes AIDS, called HIV, are not sick and don't have any symptoms (even though they can still pass the virus on to other people). That's probably what they meant at school: you can't tell if someone is infected with HIV just by looking at him or her."

Assuming That Sex Causes AIDS

Teen comment: "I don't think I'm ever gonna get married or have sex—it's too dangerous."

Your response: "Sex doesn't cause AIDS. Two people who do not have HIV can have sexual intercourse with each other for the rest of their lives and never get AIDS. Only if HIV is already in a man's semen or a woman's vaginal fluids can sexual intercourse pass on HIV. That's why a lot of couples decide to be tested for HIV before they begin an intimate relationship."

Feeling Isolated from the Epidemic

Teen comment: "AIDS has nothing to do with me, so there's nothing I can do about AIDS."

Your response: "Because AIDS is an epidemic, everyone in your generation has to deal with it. There is something you can do about it: you can protect yourself by [depending on your family values] abstaining from sex while you're a teenager [or practicing safer sex by always using a condom]. And, very important, you can make a difference by having compassion for those who are infected."

Assuming That AIDS Is Found Only in the Big Cities or Among Certain High-Risk Groups

Teen comment: "I don't have anything to worry about. Nobody in my school is gay or shoots drugs."

Your response: "People used to think that only junkies and gay men got AIDS, but now we know that that isn't true. Anyone, regardless of age, gender, sexual orientation, race, or city can become infected with HIV. There's no such thing as a special group at risk for AIDS, but there are risky behaviors that will spread HIV to anyone: things like sharing intravenous needles, and that includes the athletes who are using steroids and the kids who are giving each other tattoos and doing body piercing. It also includes have unprotected vaginal, anal, or oral sex."

Worrying That HIV Can Spread Through Casual Contact

Teen comment: "Kevin's mother told us that the rumors about Karl having AIDS are really true! I'm not sitting anywhere near him on the bus anymore."

Your response: "If Karl has the virus that causes AIDS, I feel very bad for him, but fortunately, you don't have to worry about sitting next to him. The only way you can get HIV from Karl is by sharing intravenous needles with him or by having unprotected sex with him. Otherwise, there's absolutely nothing to worry about. It's more risky for Karl to sit next to you: if he catches a cold or flu from you, it can make him very, very sick. Be sure to tell your friends not to worry about getting close to Karl."

Feeling Uncomfortable About Practicing Safer Sex

Teen comment: "Everyone says to avoid AIDS by avoiding unprotected sex, but I don't think that's so easy to do."

Your response: "A lot of things you'll do to protect your life won't be so easy, but sometimes they're necessary. Remember that you are an important person, and taking care of yourself should be a priority on your list. Participating in unprotected sex is treating yourself badly, and anyone who says he loves you but tries to get you to do something that might badly affect the rest of your life is lying to you. Loving someone means caring about what happens to her."

Missing the Relationship Between Substance Abuse and HIV

Teen comment: "I heard someone say that drinking alcohol increases your risk of getting AIDS. That's sounds ridiculous to me. You can't get AIDS from alcohol."

Your response: "You're right that you won't get the AIDS virus from alcohol, but it is true that alcohol can increase your risk of getting AIDS. Using alcohol or drugs affects your ability to think straight. So some people might do things like have unprotected sex or share intravenous needles, which they wouldn't do if they weren't high. Also, alcohol and drugs lower your resistance to disease and infection, so the body is more apt to pick up HIV if it comes in contact with it."

Worrying That HIV Can Spread Through Contact Sports

Teen comment: "I don't know if I want to go out for the wrestling team this year. Some of the kids say that HIV can spread through sweat."

Your response: "I can see why that would worry you. Let me tell you what I've read about it: it's true that HIV might be found in the sweat of some people with the HIV infection. But according to the experts who study this kind of thing, it would be in such small amounts that it poses no significant risk to others. You know I would never encourage you to do anything that would put you at risk, but I honestly believe that you can play any sport you want without worrying. Of all the AIDS cases in the world, none has been traced to contact sports."

Worrying About Kissing

Teen comment: "Casey says she still French kisses even though she knows HIV can be in saliva. How disgusting."

Your response: "Whether or not to French kiss is, of course, a personal choice, but I wouldn't worry too much about Casey. Although HIV is found in small amounts in saliva, researchers have said that you would have to swallow about a gallon of a person's saliva in order to get enough HIV to be become infected. To be on the very safe side, some people say that if you have braces, or cuts or sores in your mouth, it's probably better not to kiss in a way that exchanges large amounts of saliva."

Not Knowing About Anonymous Testing

Teen comment: "I think a lot of kids don't get tested for HIV because they don't want their parents to get all crazy and start asking a lot of questions about their sex lives."

Your response: "You're probably right, but kids should know that they can be tested without their parents knowing anything about it.

There are AIDS hotline numbers teens can call [such as the ones at the end of this chapter] that will tell them where they can go near their own home for an anonymous test. That means that no one will know their name or who they are. When they go for the test, they will be assigned a number; no one will ever ask their name."

HOW NOT TO TALK ABOUT AIDS

There are certain responses that are guaranteed to kill conversations with teenagers—you can almost hear them slamming closed the doors of communication. Read the following mistakes a parent might make when talking about HIV/AIDS. Then when you talk to your teens, think about these blunders before your speak.

Mistake: Lecturing or talking for more than a minute without letting your teen join in the conversation.
"You know, no one is exactly sure how AIDS started, but there are some researchers who believe that the virus originated in central Africa. There are many people in Africa with AIDS, and the theory is . . .," and on and on and on.

Mistake: Putting stark facts before an understanding of feelings.
"Don't be silly. There's nothing to be afraid of if you don't shoot drugs or have sex."

Mistake: Interrupting the teen's point to correct a factual error not essential to the conversation.
"It's not the 'acquired immuno virus,' it's 'acquired immunodeficiency virus.' The deficiency is very important to the name because it . . .," blah, blah, blah.

Mistake: Presenting a viewpoint as if it were fact without giving the teen a chance to respond or voice her own feelings.

"I don't care what anybody says, people who have AIDS have only themselves to blame."

Mistake: Interrupting a teen with a harsh put-down when you don't agree with his point of view.

"What a stupid thing to say. You've got a lot to learn."

Mistake: Giving advice with information that the teen will know is blatantly wrong.

"I don't want you drinking out of the water fountains at school or holding onto the stair banisters. You have no way of knowing if someone with HIV has used them."

TALKING TO TEENS WHEN YOU DON'T KNOW THE ANSWER

It's unlikely that you can know every answer to every question your kids might come up with about HIV/AIDS, but it's important to be as informed as possible so that you can offer helpful advice and set them straight when their information is way off base. If the answers to your own questions are not included in this chapter, contact your doctor, the library, or one of the free resources listed at the end of this chapter. You and your teen both need to know the facts.

In the end, your main objective when you talk to your teen about HIV/AIDS should be to dispel myths, give facts, and teach compassion for those infected. (See "Sexually Transmitted Diseases" for more information on prevention.)

RESOURCES

The Centers for Disease Control and Prevention are a reliable source of information about HIV and AIDS. The counselors who answer their National AIDS Hotline phones can answer questions as well as refer you to organizations in your area that deal with the issues you're concerned about.

National AIDS Hotline
(800) 342-AIDS
Twenty-four hours a day, every day

National AIDS Hotline in Spanish
(800) 344-SIDA
8:00 A.M. to 2:00 A.M., every day

National AIDS Hotline for the Hearing Impaired
(800) 243-7889
10:00 A.M. to 10:00 P.M., Monday through Friday

Teens Teaching AIDS Prevention
(800) 234-TEEN
4:00 P.M. to 8:00 P.M., Monday through Saturday

A switchboard operated by teenagers who have been trained to answer questions about HIV and AIDS.

FOR FURTHER READING

Acker, Loren. *AIDS-Proofing Your Kids*. Hillsboro, Oreg.: Beyond Words, 1992.

Froman, Paul Kent. *After You Say Goodbye: When Someone You Love Dies of AIDS*. San Francisco: Chronicle Books, 1992.

Garwood, Ann, and Ben Melnick. *What Everyone Can Do to Fight AIDS*. San Francisco: Jossey-Bass, 1995.

Especially for Teens

Ford, Michael Thomas. *100 Questions and Answers About AIDS: A Guide for Young People*. Old Tappan, N.J.: Macmillan, 1992.

Hein, Karen, and Theresa Foy DiGeronimo. *AIDS: Trading Fears for Facts: A Guide for Young People*. (3rd ed.) New York: Consumer Reports Books, 1993.

Sex, Contraception, and **Pregnancy**

As they neared the supermarket checkout counter, thirteen-year-old Katlyn threw a magazine into the shopping cart. "Mom, can you buy this?" she asked.

Rosemary looked at the magazine; the headlines screamed, "No-Fail Love Secrets!" "Sexy Scents to Keep Your Guy Hot," and "Killer Fashions to Turn His Head." Was this the stuff she wanted her daughter reading? Was this what other thirteen-year-olds were into? Rosemary bought the magazine to avoid a scene about a subject she wasn't willing to discuss in the supermarket, but she felt ill at ease and even a bit angry.

That night Rosemary told her husband about the incident. "From TV to movies to music to magazines, these kids are bombarded with sexual messages," she complained. "What are they supposed to think? What am I supposed to say?"

Teenagers will always be curious about sex—this is natural and good. The problem with this curiosity is that teens are physically capable of having sexual intercourse and of conceiving children long before they are emotionally mature enough to form a close or stable sexual relationship. This is why they need your help and guidance through these confusing years of peer pressure, mixed messages, and raging hormones.

WHY YOU SHOULD TALK

Many adults reason, "No one talked to me about sex, and I made out just fine. So why should I talk to my own kids when it makes them and me feel so uncomfortable?" There are four good reasons to talk:

1. Everybody else is talking: TV, movies, music, MTV, magazines, and friends. Our teenagers are exposed to sexual language and activities that do not give them a true picture of sexual joy and responsibility. They need us to supply the balance.
2. Sexual activity among teenagers today begins at an earlier age than even a generation ago and is more prevalent. A recent survey found that 56 percent of American teenage girls and 73 percent of American teenage boys have had sexual intercourse by their eighteenth birthday.
3. The potential risk of contracting sexually transmitted diseases (STDs), including AIDS, has escalated dramatically. (See "HIV/AIDS" and "Sexually Transmitted Diseases" for more information.)
4. The incidence of unwanted teenage pregnancy has jumped twofold over the past twenty years. More than one million adolescents become pregnant each year in the United States. That's about three thousand a day. Before they leave their teens, four out of ten girls will become pregnant—most of them unintentionally.

Looking at these statistics, you can see why teens need to talk about sex, contraception, and pregnancy. Your goal is to make them willing to talk to *you*.

BEFORE YOU TALK

Before you bring up the subject of sex, contraception, or pregnancy, explore your own feelings first. If you're comfortable talking about these topics, you'll send that message to your children. They'll know from the tone of your voice, from your body language, and from your openness that these are not embarrassing, taboo subjects.

But if you're uneasy about discussing these aspects of human sexuality, you'll communicate that too. Although it's impossible to suddenly make yourself feel relaxed and comfortable about these issues, that doesn't mean you can clam up and keep your fingers crossed that your kids will be OK. Studies show that kids who feel they can talk to their parents about sex because their parents speak openly and listen attentively to them actually engage in less sexual activity and high-risk behavior than kids who have learned not to broach the subject. So even if you're uncomfortable, it's still important to talk. You might open the door to discussion by admitting your feelings. You might say something like, "I'm uncomfortable talking about sex because my parents never talked to me about it. But I want us to be able to talk about anything—including sex—so please come to me if you have any questions. If I don't know the answer, I'll find out."

Also, before you talk to your teens, make sure you're informed. You might want to take a look at some books on sexuality (especially the ones written for teens) so that when you do talk, you'll have your facts straight and won't embarrass yourself or your teen (a sure way to end all further discussions about sexuality!).

Keep in mind that even after you've examined your own beliefs and brushed up on the birds and bees, there may be topics you're not completely knowledgeable about. That's OK. What you know is less important than the fact that your children know you are willing to listen and talk.

WHEN TO TALK

Ideally, you have been talking to your kids about sexuality since they were very young. By age five, children should be familiar with the correct terms for sexual body parts; by age six to eight they should be able to correctly use biological terms like vulva, vagina, breast, penis, and testicles; by nine to eleven, children should know the facts about how babies are born and how the reproductive cycle works. With this background, it's easier to talk to teenagers about their own sexuality. However, even if you've never before mentioned the subject, you should promise yourself that *now* you will start talking to your teen.

It is best to start talking before your kids begin a serious relationship. This keeps the conversation objective and makes the give-and-take of dialogue much easier to accomplish. It also provides a foundation of understanding you can use when your teen does have a steady girlfriend or boyfriend. That's the way it works ideally.

Still, it's very common to start thinking about the Big Talk when you realize your teen is falling in love. Once this happens, you certainly should talk about sex, contraception, and pregnancy, but keep in mind that the going can get tough. Everything you say will be weighed against the feelings for the new love. Every opinion may be taken as a personal attack. Emotions are raw. The best way both to respect your teen's vulnerable state and to still get your message across is to use teachable moments that throw a bit of objectivity back into the subject.

Look for Teachable Moments

The news seems to be filled with heartbreaking stories about young couples and frightened girls who deliver their babies in public toilets, garages, or motel rooms and then leave them there to die. Sadly, this can be the consequence of having no one to talk to. You can use these kinds of news stories to plant seeds and open dialogue. You might comment, "This girl must have been so frightened. Why do you think she couldn't talk to her parents about her pregnancy? Why do you think her boyfriend didn't even know she was pregnant? It's too bad she didn't know about all the agencies set up to help young girls just like her." You can also use these kinds of tragedies to help deliver your own message: "I want you to know right now that no matter what happens in your life, it will never be so terrible that you can't talk to me about it—but let's not wait for a tragedy to talk."

These kinds of teachable moments are found everywhere:

- On TV shows where the characters jump in and out of bed with a different person each episode: "How come nobody ever gets pregnant or gets an STD on this show?"
- On a shopping trip to the mall, where you and your teen see a young couple using a bench as if it were a private bedroom: "Do you think making love should be a public sport?"
- In the lyrics of songs that encourage free or abusive sex: "I don't agree with what that song says. Do you?"

- In magazine headlines that scream "How to Be a Great Kisser": "I wonder . . . can a magazine article really tell you how to kiss?"

Teachable moments are all around you. No longer can parents use the excuse, "I just can't seem to find the right moment to talk about the birds and bees." Those moments are flung at us from all directions. It's up to us to grab onto them and use them.

WHAT TO TALK ABOUT

When you talk to your teens about sex, don't worry that you'll put ideas in their head or give them information they don't need now. The ideas are already there; teens just need help sorting them out and finding a way to make them fit in their lives. And if they don't need the information now, they will eventually. You won't be around to give the facts and your values when they move out of the house—now is the time.

There's a lot to cover. To know where to begin, you might contact the science and health department at your teen's school and find out if they have a curriculum that covers human sexuality, reproduction, and contraception. This will give you insight into the information they already have (or don't have).

If your teen is learning about human sexuality in school, contact the teacher and explain that you would like to know when these issues are covered in class so that you can talk about them with your child at home. Don't worry that you're bothering the teacher. Teachers pray for a parent who wants to continue these kinds of classroom discussions at home.

SEX, CONTRACEPTION, AND PREGNANCY

The Facts

If your school system does not include human sexuality in the curriculum, your teen needs your help to learn the basic facts of reproduction and contraception. If a sit-down talk is too uncomfortable for you or your teen, then at the very least get a good book (like the ones listed at the end of this chapter) written specifically for teens. Give your teen the book, hold direct eye contact, and say:

"I want you to have the right answers to all your questions about sex, so I've bought you this book. I also want you to know that I'd be glad to talk to you about anything you read in here or to answer any other questions you might have."

Even if your teen protests and blushes and pushes the book back into your hands, make him keep it. There is no doubt that one year from now that book will be worn and ragged from use.

Contraception

Before you talk about contraception, you need to think carefully about what you want to say. If your personal or religious beliefs do not condone the use of contraceptive methods to prevent pregnancy, sit down and explain this to your teens. Tell them how you feel and why you have these beliefs. Then have a heart-to-heart that explains the importance of abstinence for young teens. Tell them that this is the safest and only truly effective method of birth control and that it's not an uncommon thing to do. The news is full of stories about today's teens giving peer support for abstinence by forming organized groups, taking pledges, and spreading the word that abstinence is smart. Don't be afraid to talk about it in your house.

If you want your children to use contraceptive methods when they become sexually active, tell them. In a survey of teens who said their parents had talked to them about sex, only 46 percent said their parents ever mentioned birth control. If you consider premarital sex inevitable, don't overlook the value of bringing up the subject of contraception. Your teens can't read your mind and are very unlikely to ask your opinion on this subject. If you're more comfortable keeping the discussion objective, express your feelings when reading the news. When you see an article about an unmarried, pregnant teen, say:

"I always wonder why these teenagers don't use contraceptives. If they feel they're old enough to have intercourse, they should be old enough to take care of their health too. What do you think?"

This will get the discussion going.

The ideal time to talk about contraception is before it is needed. Don't worry that talking about safer sex practices will encourage sex. It tells your teen that you realize he or she is a sexual being who someday will want to have a loving and safe relationship with another person. And when that day comes, you'll want him or her to know the facts. You might say:

"You may not feel you're ready for this information, and I don't want you to have sexual intercourse while you're still a teenager, but I'd like to share it so that when you do need it, you'll know the facts."

If you know your teen is already sexually active, then it's absolutely vital to talk about contraception and to ensure that your teen is using a safe method of birth control. Don't worry that this kind of discussion will condone the sexual activity; you can make it clear that you are adamantly against early sex before a person is ready to take on the responsibilities of pregnancy, STDs, and AIDS, *but* because your child feels differently, in the very least he or she can take the responsibility to stay healthy. Once a teen becomes sexually active, this isn't a discussion that can be postponed. One-half of all premarital teenage pregnancies occur in the first six months after intercourse has begun, and 10 percent occur in the first month.

The method of contraception for boys is the condom. They should know how to use it correctly; almost all the books on sexuality written for boys include simple illustrated guides. Let your son know that he can buy condoms in any drugstore, no questions asked.

For girls, the issue of contraception is more complex because of the variety of choices. Your daughter needs professional counseling to help her understand the use of the pill, the diaphragm, spermicidal creams and foams, and so on. Your role is to ensure that she knows there are ways to prevent pregnancy. Tell her that any girl age sixteen and older can legally receive advice from a family doctor or from a birth control clinic without the parents' knowledge or consent.

Whatever your personal feelings, sexually active boys and girls need to be told, "If you're old enough to have sex, you must be mature enough to know how to use contraceptives."

TALKING ABOUT FAMILY VALUES

Whether or not your teen's school offers a program on human sexuality, all teens need to know how the facts of life fit into their family's value system. Learning that sperm fertilizes an egg and makes a baby doesn't tell a teen anything about the lifelong ramifications of premarital intercourse. That's your job.

Communicate your values. This will give your teens a foundation to work from as they struggle to figure out what they value and how they want to behave. If you believe teens are too young for sexual relationships, say so. Your teen may breathe a sigh of relief when she finds out that you support what she is feeling and struggling with. Apparently teens aren't getting the message that they don't have to have sex; 54 percent of the sexually active teens interviewed for a study out of the University of Nebraska said that they had engaged in sex when they did not want to. How will your teen know the whole world doesn't think rushing into sex is good unless you speak up? TV, movies, music, and friends are all conspiring to convince young people that teenage sex is the norm. Hearing the other side from you can be a great comfort (but don't expect your teen to admit this).

Communicate your values without apology—there's no guarantee that you can prevent sexual activity or irresponsible unprotected sex, but you don't have to condone it.

HOW TO TALK

Here are some pointers on how to talk to your teen about sex.

- Keep the door open. Even if your teenager resists all attempts to discuss issues of sexuality, don't give up. Make sure they know, "Any sexual feeling, issue, or thought that you have can always be discussed calmly between us. That doesn't mean that we'll always agree. But it does mean that I love you."
- Don't let your conversations about sex always focus on negatives, warnings, fears, and prohibitions. Try to make a proportion

of your discussions positive. Remember that sex does not mean only intercourse. It means talking to members of the opposite sex, kidding, dating, kissing, caring, and learning to enjoy romantic feelings. This fact gets easily lost today when the people on TV and in movies meet for the first time, go to dinner, and then go to bed. Kids need to know that in real life, there's time to get to know each other—time to hold hands, go bowling, see a movie, or just talk. This is an important and fun part of a caring relationship.

• Use your own teen stories. Share your mistakes, laugh at your good times. Let your teen know that there are many things about sexuality that are natural, normal, healthy, and fun.

• Don't trivialize your child's romantic or sexual feelings. Instead encourage him or her to be open about feelings, attitudes, romantic interests, and relationships.

• Learn to listen. Often say, "Tell me more about that." "How do *you* feel about that?"

• Don't jump to conclusions. If you find a condom in the jacket pocket, stay calm and think before your speak. An explosive reaction—"I demand to know if you're having sex"—will kill an ideal opportunity to find out what's going on with your teen. There are many reasons a teen might have a condom in his or her pocket, or a sex manual under the bed, or birth control pills in her pocketbook. Give your teen a chance to explain and yourself the chance to listen. By remaining calm and listening attentively, you'll create a safe moment for honest talk. You may not like the honest answer, but at least the door will be open for further discussion.

Speak Loudly Without Saying a Word

When you talk to your kids about sensitive and sometimes embarrassing subjects, your body language can speak louder than your words. The words "I want you to know that you can talk to me about anything at all" give two very different messages when a parent says them while sitting face-to-face, leaning forward with direct eye contact and another says them while sitting across the room leafing through the newspaper.

When you talk to your teens about sex, contraception, and pregnancy, keep these basic rules of body language in mind:

- Distance: sit within three feet of your teen.
- Position: sit, leaning forward toward your teen. Don't cross your arms or your legs.
- Eye contact: look at your teen and encourage him or her to look back at you.
- Facial expression: let the expression on your face support the words. Frowning and smirking are negative signals; smiles, a head nod, and an attentive look send positive signals.

PERSONAL AND CONTROVERSIAL

Some issues of teen sex, contraception, and pregnancy are very personal and even controversial and are viewed differently by different families. We recognize this and expect that there may be some things you will want to add to or delete from the information given in this chapter. We have included a broad view of teen sexuality so that if you choose to talk about it, you will have the information you need. Whatever you decide, you should make an effort to talk about your feelings and beliefs openly and honestly. Let your teens know where you stand, use teachable moments to reinforce your message, and always leave the door open for them to come to you.

FOR FURTHER READING

Langford, Laurie. *The Big Talk: Talking to Your Teens About Sex and Dating.* New York: Wiley, 1998.

Especially for Teens

Kelly, Gary. *Sex and Sense: A Contemporary Guide for Teenagers.* Hauppauge, N.Y.: Barrons Juveniles, 1993.

Solin, Sabrina, and Paula Elbirt. *The Seventeen Guide to Sex and Your Body.* New York: Aladdin Paperbacks, 1996.

Stoppard, Miriam, and Sally Artz. *Sex Ed: Growing Up, Relationships, and Sex.* New York: DK Publishing, 1997.

Sexually Transmitted Diseases

Sixteen-year-old Kyle was so relieved. He had been worried sick because he had had a discharge from his penis and a burning sensation during urination that was driving him crazy. He was just about ready to tell his parents when the symptoms disappeared. What a relief!

What a shame—Kyle still has a sexually transmitted disease (STD), even though the acute symptoms have subsided. Without treatment, this disease will stay in his body and be passed on to future sex partners. And if he does not get tested and treated, he may end up with permanent damage to his reproductive organs. Like millions of other teens, Kyle thinks he's perfectly healthy, but he's now infected with an STD, and his ignorance is jeopardizing his health and contributing to the epidemic.

It is not easy to talk to teens about STDs—it's a subject that both kids and parents feel shy about. But because there are so many kids like Kyle out there, it's not a choice—it's a must.

HOW TO TALK ABOUT STDs

You should talk to your teens about sexually transmitted diseases the same way you talk about any private, potentially embarrassing, subject: with a great deal of sensitivity, but also with perseverance. You'll need sensitivity to tune into your teen's feelings and comfort level, and you'll need perseverance to get out the facts even when your teen asks you to stop. When you broach the subject, you might say something like this: "I hope this won't embarrass you, but I think we need to talk about all the STDs like syphilis and herpes that are around so that you'll have the right information when you need it."

Don't be put off if you find yourself in a one-sided conversation. Your teen may not jump in to offer information or to share stories. That's OK. Get your facts straight and expect to do most of the talking.

WHY YOU SHOULD TALK ABOUT STDs

We all should talk to our teens about STDs because these infections include more than twenty different diseases that affect some three million teenagers in the United States every year. That means one in four sexually active teens contracts an STD before leaving high school. We should talk to our teens because 90 percent of them are no longer virgins when they leave high school. (Even if you are sure your teen is not sexually active now, it is very likely that he or she will be at some point and will need to know the facts then.) We should talk to them because it is unlikely that they will talk to us. We should talk to them about all STDs because the fear of HIV/AIDS has taken focus away from the others. Many teens now get tested for HIV, without thinking about the other infections that are epidemic among sexually active people. This is a sensitive and private topic that is embarrassing to bring out in the open. But you have to keep in mind that silence has far-reaching ramifications that go far beyond simple embarrassment. Millions of people take diseases from their teen years into bed with their mates later on.

Consider the effects of chlamydia alone (the most common STD in the United States, affecting an estimated three to ten million people each year): 20 percent of infected males and 75 percent of infected females have no symptoms of this STD, but if chlamydia is left untreated, it can cause infections in the testicles and the tubes, pelvic inflammatory disease, sterility, and permanent damage to reproductive organs. Babies born to infected women can become infected themselves and develop eye infections and pneumonia. We cannot let ignorance so severely endanger the health of our children.

WHEN TO TALK ABOUT STDs

Because you'll probably be doing most of the talking, you need to find a time when your teen will listen, a time when there's nothing else going on. Choose a time when you and your teen can sit down together and talk uninterrupted for at least twenty minutes. (This leaves time in case your teen has questions he or she feels comfortable asking.) Choose a time when your teen is in a receptive mood (not distracted with school or friend problems). Choose a time when the household is less likely to be hectic and when you can take the phone off the hook. You might try talking while riding in the car—this gives you a captive audience. These things make it easier for you to hold your teenagers' attention on a subject that makes them want to bolt out the door.

There is no one perfect time to bring up this subject. But you might consider these ideas.

Immediately

If you know or suspect that your teen is sexually active, now is the time you must talk about STDs. There's no reason to believe that your teen will be lucky enough to be sexually active and avoid an infectious disease. Luck has nothing to do with this. Sexually active people stay healthy when they have the information they need to make mature choices.

After School

In many schools, discussion of STDs is part of the health curriculum. Call your child's school and find out if and when this subject is discussed. (You can do this without embarrassing yourself if you ask for a health curriculum for your child's grade. This will give you all the information you need without asking for it directly.) If you find that STDs are on the list, you'll want to time your discussion to match the classroom discussions. When the subject is already on the table at school, it's easy to ask, "What are you discussing about STDs? Which ones have you talked about? Which one do you think is the worst? Do you think any kids in your school might have an STD?" Reinforcing the facts at home will help your teen appreciate the seriousness of this problem. You can ask your teen to let you know when the subject comes up (keeping in mind that this is not a very reliable tactic), or you can ask the health teacher to let you know when this subject will be presented to the class.

While They're Still Young Enough to Listen

If you believe your teen has abstained from sexual activity (both oral and genital) during middle school and high school, your conversation about STDs might be postponed for a while. But don't forget that your teen will be a sexually active person at some time and will need this information. Young teens are much more likely to listen to you than older ones, so don't wait too long to have this conversation. Most experts recommend that all children know about the dangers of STDs by age twelve or thirteen—this is especially important in this time of AIDS.

WHAT YOU SHOULD TALK ABOUT

We don't think it's best to sit down and go over each and every known STD, listing the symptoms, complications, and treatments for each one. This comes off too much like a lecture and not a discussion. Instead, give your teens the general information they need to be aware, cautious, and safe. You might begin by offering your teen the chance to talk about what he or she already knows.

You might ask: "Did you ever hear anybody at school talk about a medical problem with nicknames like 'syph,' 'VD,' 'clap,' 'strain,' 'dose,' or 'old Joe'?"

If your teen says, "Yeah," be supportive: "It's good to hear that teens are aware of sexually transmitted diseases. I was surprised to read the other day that some three million teens are infected!"

If your teen says no, don't drop the subject. Say: "I'm surprised. These are all nicknames for sexually transmitted diseases that are very common among teenagers. I read the other day that some three million teens are infected with these diseases!"

Then continue: "There are quite a few of these diseases, and you can have more than one at a time. Maybe you know their medical names: chlamydia, gonorrhea, syphilis, genital herpes, human papilloma virus (HPV), and human immunodeficiency virus (HIV)."

If your teen is turned off by this topic, present your reason for bringing it up: "STDs infect millions of people every year. Because I love you, I want to be sure you know about this epidemic and know how to keep yourself safe. Some of this you may already know. Some may be new information. Just listen and store it all away for when you need it."

Now the subject is on the table. If your teen is open to the conversation, follow his or her lead by listening carefully and filling in the blanks with the following information about transmission, symptoms, treatment, and prevention when you see that it's needed.

Transmission

Tell your teen: "Sex alone does not cause STDs (although a lot of people think this). You can become infected with an STD only if you have sex (oral, anal, or genital) with an infected person.

Symptoms

Tell your teen: "Anyone who is sexually active should suspect an STD and see a doctor if he or she has any of these symptoms:

Discharge from the vagina, penis, or rectum
Pain or burning during urination or intercourse
Pain in the abdomen (women), testicles (men), and buttocks and legs (both)
Blisters, open sores, warts, rash, or swelling in the genital area, sex organs, or mouth

Flu-like symptoms, including fever, headache, aching muscles, or swollen glands

"Keep these in mind, but also remember that some STDs have *no* symptoms. Others have symptoms that disappear without treatment, but this doesn't mean the disease is gone. People who feel healthy believe they don't have STDs, but that's not necessarily true."

Be sure to emphasize: "Many people with STDs don't even know they have them. Any teen who is sexually active may carry one (or more) sexually transmitted diseases."

Treatment
Tell your teen: "STDs are a serious problem that must be treated. The treatment depends on the type of STD: most are bacterial infections and require a prescription antibiotic; others are viral and have no cure, but they are not deadly, and the symptoms can be treated with medications. HIV, as I'm sure you know, has no cure and is deadly." (See "HIV/AIDS" for ideas for discussing this STD.)

Because so many teens don't seek medical care when they notice symptoms of STDs, tell your teens:

"Left untreated, STDs can cause very serious medical problems including

Tubal pregnancies, sometimes fatal to the mother and always fatal to the unborn child
Death or severe damage to a baby born to an infected woman
Sterility
Infertility

Cancer of the cervix in women
Damage to other parts of the body, including the heart, kid-
   neys, and brain
Death
Blindness
Arthritis
Severe mental illness"

This is scary information, but it often is not scary enough to make teens open up and ask for help. Many teens who worry they may be infected respond to this kind of information by worrying more but doing nothing. This is a time to respect teenagers' need for sexual privacy. If you suspect that your teen does not feel free to confide in you, put your child's health above personal pride. Inform him or her:

"In all states, minors can be tested, diagnosed, and treated for STDs without parental consent or knowledge. If you should ever need medical care and feel very uncomfortable telling me or going to our family doctor, you can call the local board of health, and someone there can refer you to a doctor or the nearest STD or adolescent health clinic for anonymous medical attention. I tell you this hoping that you will come to me first, but what's most important is that you take care of your health."

Prevention
The problem with giving teens these facts is that they make sex sound dangerous and dirty. The goal of your discussion should be to help your teen see sex as a safe and natural human expression between two people who love each other and do not wish to pass on sexually transmitted diseases.

If you believe that your teen is not sexually active and you encourage abstinence during the teen years, tell your teen how you feel:

"The responsible and safe way for teenagers to avoid STDs is through abstinence from sexual intercourse. Kids who abstain from sex do not have to spend one minute worrying about pregnancy and disease."

However, if you suspect your teen is sexually active, or if you want to give your teen information she will need when she does become sexually active, your discussion of prevention should go beyond talking about abstinence. Tell your teen:

- "Don't have casual sex with people you don't know. Casual sex is serious self-destruction. You have sex with everyone your partner has ever had sex with. If you don't know this person, you should assume he or she has had sex with lots of other people he or she did not know either. The chances are that people who have casual sex carry STDs."
- "Stick to one steady partner. The more partners a person has, the higher the risk of getting an STD."
- "Whenever you have sex, use a condom. A condom acts as a barrier or wall to keep blood, semen, and vaginal fluids from passing from one person to the other during intercourse. These fluids can carry the germs of STDs. If you don't use a condom, the germs can pass from the infected partner to the uninfected partner."

Be sure to emphasize: "Condoms do not guarantee that you won't get a sexually transmitted disease, but most experts believe that the risk of getting AIDS and other sexually transmitted diseases can be greatly reduced if a condom is used properly. In other words, sex with condoms isn't totally safe sex, but it is less risky sex."

Make sure your teen knows the basics:

- Only new condoms are strong.
- Old or heat-damaged condoms will not work. (The glove compartment or wallet is not the place to store condoms.)
- Condoms are not reusable.
- A new condom must be worn if partners have anal and then vaginal intercourse.
- Condoms must be worn correctly on an erect penis.
- Condoms can be bought in any pharmacy without a prescription.

When you talk about prevention, you're really talking about responsibility. Make sure your teens know:

"It is the responsibility of every sexually active male and female to make sure that he or she is protected against STDs and to get routine medical care. If you think you and your partner should be using condoms but your partner refuses, then you should say NO to sex with that person."

Myths

Your teen could probably tell you hundreds of ways to prevent STDs; every generation mixes and mingles all the old remedies and comes up with a few new ones of its own. Let your teen know that most "home remedies," including these popular recipes, do not prevent or treat STDs:

Contraceptives such as the Pill, diaphragms, sponges, and creams

Douching (This can actually push infectious microorganisms
farther into the vagina.)

Bathing (Washing the male genitals may help flush away
STD-causing microorganisms, but not always. Bathing is
not at all effective for females.)

Antibiotics that might be left in the medicine cabinet from an
old case of strep throat (Antibiotics prescribed for other illnesses should not be used as treatment for STDs.)

Having only oral or anal sex (Both can transmit STDs.)

That's it. If your teens have this basic information about STDs,
they are less likely to risk infection. In addition, just knowing that
this is a subject you know about and are willing to talk about will
give them someone to turn to with their worries and concerns.

RESOURCES

STD Hotline
(800) 227-8922
For quick answers to all questions about STDs.

FOR FURTHER READING

Especially for Teens
Brodman, Michael, and others. *Straight Talk About Sexually Transmitted
Diseases*. New York: Facts on File, 1993.

Woods, Samuel. *Everything You Need to Know About Sexually Transmitted
Diseases*. New York: Rosen Publishing Group, 1997.

Tattoos and **Body Piercing**

Jody had been talking about her new boyfriend for weeks. Everything about him seemed perfect: he was kind, considerate, fun, and caring. "So why won't you bring him around the house?" asked her mother.

"He's shy," Jody mumbled.

"No, he's not," blurted out her younger brother. "He's got a dozen rings hanging off his face. That's why she doesn't want you to see him." Case solved.

Jody was afraid that her parents would get a bad impression of her boyfriend if they saw that his nose, eyebrow, tongue, ear, cheek, and lip were "decorated" with rings. And she was probably right. But more to the point, finding out about Jody's boyfriend made her parents most concerned about Jody. They knew that if she found body piercing attractive on her friends, it wouldn't be long before she wanted it for herself. It was time to talk.

NO LONGER A FAD ON THE FRINGE

Body piercing and tattooing are no longer initiation rites for street gangs or the eccentric trappings of lunatic rock bands. They're

121

mainstream American teen. Belly button rings, tongue barbells, and butterfly tattoos are as common today as love beads and incense were in the sixties. They have shed their outlaw image and have been mass-marketed to the impressionable teen by music videos, music idols, and models.

WHAT'S THE BIG DEAL?

This fad is of more concern to many parents than torn knees in jeans or blue streaks in the hair because it permanently affects the body and can cause a host of medical complications and problems. Taking a good look at the facts about tattooing and body piercing is the first place to start as you prepare to talk to your teen about this fad. This will help you decide where you stand on the matter before you're cornered, and, as in all things, when you know what you're talking about, you're more likely to bring your teen into a meaningful dialogue.

TATTOOING

Tattooing is a permanent method of decorating the skin by inserting colored inks or dyes under the surface of the skin with a needle or other sharp instrument. This your teen knows, but he or she may not know the details about the tattooing procedure, the pain involved, the care required afterward to prevent infection, the removal procedures, or the legal age requirements for this form of body decoration.

Tattooing Procedure

Most simple tattoos take at least an hour to complete, and large or fancy ones take several hours. Whatever the design or size, the process can be extremely painful, and the pain lasts throughout the procedure. In fact, it is not uncommon for a person to throw up or even faint while getting a tattoo. (An interesting tidbit: tattooing the skin right over bones, such as the collarbone or ankle-bone, tends to be more painful than other areas.) Because unrelenting pain is tough for even the most hardened biker to bear, a responsible tattoo artist works for only three or four hours at the most during one visit. (It's sometimes a good idea to encourage your teen to watch a friend go through this procedure before deciding if this kind of body decoration is worth the physical trauma.)

After all this, tattoos do not keep their original bright colors—they will fade over time, giving them a worn-out look. To keep the sharp appearance, some tattoo artists use india ink, which is very black and does not fade. The down side is that india ink contains poison. Although it probably won't kill your daughter, it can make her extremely ill. It can also prevent her from having children, or it may cause birth defects in the children she does have. This is certainly something to know about.

Aftercare of a Tattoo

The care of a new tattoo takes time and patience but is absolutely necessary to avoid infections, scarring, and ruined tattoos. The tattoo must be kept bandaged for the first twenty-four hours. After the bandage comes off, antibacterial ointment must be applied to the area three times daily for two to three weeks. After the tattoo scabs, it becomes extremely dry, so it's important to keep it moist for the first month or two using a moisturizing lotion every day. Your teen cannot go swimming for at least two weeks after getting a tattoo, and he must avoid direct sunlight for two to four weeks because sunlight will fade the colors. (Obviously, summertime—the time kids most often think about decorating their skin—is not the best time of year for a tattoo.)

Tattoo Removal

Your teen should also know the details about tattoo removal. Granted, all teens have a hard time imagining life even five years in the future, but before they plead for body art they may grow to hate when the fad passes, they should know the facts. There are two options for someone who wishes to part with a tattoo. The first option is to have it covered with another tattoo. This is a popular choice for people who tattoo the name of a boyfriend or girlfriend on their body and then move on and leave this love behind. This change of heart is painful and extremely expensive. The other option is laser surgery in which a doctor uses a laser to remove the colors or pigments from the tattoo. Unfortunately, laser surgery cannot remove the ink itself from the body, so the ink will be with you for the rest of your life. Also, laser surgery doesn't make the tattoo disappear. It leaves a flesh-colored tattoo by forming a scar over your former tattoo. The cost to remove one square inch of tattoo ranges from $500 to $1,000.

Despite the pain and expense, tattoo removal is big business. In May 1994, the city government of San Jose, California, sponsored a weeklong program under which former gang members could have their tattoos removed by laser surgery without charge. The response to the program was overwhelming: more than one thousand tattoos were removed. Obviously, there are a lot of people out there who regret their decision to go for permanent body decoration.

The Law

Tattooing is not something to be done impulsively or on a whim. It is serious business. So serious that in the United States, tattooing is against the law in many communities. Where it is allowed, it is often restricted to persons at least eighteen years of age or is allowed for minors only with the consent of a parent or guardian. Find out what the law in your area says by calling your state health department.

BODY PIERCING

Body piercing is becoming very popular among teens, but it is not new. Besides being used as part of spiritual or tribal rituals throughout history, ear piercing has been fashionably popular among women in the United States since the turn of the twentieth century. In the 1980s, it became common for both women and men to have multiple piercings in their ears. Then in the 1990s, the nose, eyebrow, lip, tongue, cheek, navel, nipple, and genitals all became fashion targets for ringed and studded jewelry.

Piercing Procedure

Body piercing is not a pleasurable experience—it hurts! Most people start with an earring pierce and think that body piercing will be as simple and painless. There is a big difference. The body tissue, muscles, and nerve endings in the nose, lip, navel, nipple, and so on are not like the cartilage in the ear lobe. They are much more sensitive to pain, infection, and permanent damage.

To make the hole, the skin is marked with two dots where the needle will go in and come out. The skin is then pulled away from the body for the piercing. Usually the area will not be numbed with any kind of anesthesia, because such drugs can be administered only by a licensed medical practitioner. The intense pain of the piercing lasts only a few minutes; it is replaced with a soreness that will last for several weeks.

The average healing time for a piercing is much longer than it is for a tattoo. Nose piercings take about four to six weeks; navel piercings take four to six months. During this time, the skin around the piercing will feel tender and sensitive. Tongue piercings are particularly sore, and the tongue often swells for several days, making eating and talking almost impossible.

Aftercare

Like tattooing, piercing breaks open the skin and exposes the body to infection, so the new piercing must be kept clean at all times. The piercing site should be washed at least three times a day for as long as it takes to heal completely. Because flesh can heal onto the jewelry, the jewelry in the piercing should be turned at least three or four times a day (washing hands first). And as with tattooing, the "piercee" must avoid swimming for two weeks after being pierced (putting a crimp in vacation plans).

It can happen that the body will reject a piercing. This means it will not heal and will become infected no matter how carefully the piercing is cared for. (It's estimated that this will happen to about 50 percent of all navel piercings.) If this happens, the jewelry must be removed so that the piercing can heal and close, leaving a scar behind. But that doesn't mean the end of body piercing, because it's possible that the body will reject a piercing in one area and not react at all to another. The outcome of piercing is unpredictable and can become an expensive gamble. This is OK as long as teens know this from the start.

The Law

Right now, there is very little government regulation that applies to body piercing. Few local governments actively monitor piercing establishments or require any kind of training or licensing for piercing "artists" (although they do require licenses for all barbers). For these reasons alone, your teen needs to be on guard when even thinking about body piercing.

Removing the Piercing

Make sure your teen knows that she cannot "remove" a piercing. It is not true that if one removes the jewelry from a piercing, the opening will heal and close. Piercing puts a hole in the body. Once properly healed, the hole remains whether one puts jewelry in it or not. Pierced teens can choose to stop wearing jewelry if they grow tired of this look, but they will still have to live with a very visible, unattractive hole in their body.

WHEN THE ANSWER IS NO

After you have investigated the facts, you can say no to body piercing and tattooing. Just add it to the list:

"You do not have my approval to take illegal drugs, drink alcohol, stay out all night, or permanently alter your body with tattooing or piercing."

That's it. Bottom line. This isn't the easy option, but it certainly is an option.

Who's in Charge?

Teens like to think that they should be in complete charge of their lives—that's normal and a natural part of growing away from you. They'll tell you that you have no right to say what they can and can't do with their own bodies. They'll insist that you just want to control them, that you don't want them to grow up.

You know, however, that it's your job to stay in control of your teen. And, fortunately, the law agrees with you. That's why children under age eighteen are called minors. That's why if your child breaks the law, you can be held responsible. That's why laws—drinking age laws, driving age laws, lottery and gambling age laws, and on and on—are made to protect young people from their inflated view of personal competence. This is the world we all live in. People under eighteen are not in charge.

This hard-line approach is not cruel—it's parenting through the tough issues without giving up on what you sincerely believe is best for your children. When your kids know you won't back down, they may also use your firmness to save face. Many a teen has protested passionately and loudly only to return to her room (after slamming the door) feeling relieved. She can now blame her unreasonable and old-fashioned parents for not being allowed to do something she doesn't really want to do anyway but feels pressured to do by her peers.

Start Talking

If you know you will not allow your teen to be tattooed or pierced, don't wait for him to ask before you put your foot down. You have to let your teen know where you stand, because even in towns and cities where it's against the law, it's too easy for kids to arrive for dinner wearing a permanent tattoo or piercing. Underground tattoo and piercing parlors are popping up around the country. Piercing from head to toe occurs at parties, street fairs, virtually any social scene. Young people pierce and tattoo themselves and each other. Many a parent has been horrified to find that their son or daughter pierced the skin with a darning needle and stuck a safety pin through the hole.

Bring up the subject when you're with your teen and you both see someone wearing tattoos or rings. Without criticizing or ridiculing that person, clearly voice your feelings. Say straight out:

"I want you to know that you do not have my permission to get a tattoo or to get any part of your body pierced. Don't even think about surprising me one day with a piece of body art. You are not allowed."

Then stay open to discussion if your teen wants to talk (or protest). Let her voice her opinions, encourage her to tell you what she knows about the procedures or to discuss any friends who have already decorated themselves. You're in the driver's seat here. You can listen and talk and explain your decision, but you don't need to argue when the decision is final and nonnegotiable.

WHEN YOU'RE OPEN TO THE IDEA

You may be open to your teen's need to express himself through tattooing or body piercing and are willing to talk things over. In this case, your job is to help your teen think through this decision. Too many teens decide on impulse to be tattooed or pierced. They want to fit in, or they want to strike out against middle-class values or express a sense of daring. All of this is fine, as long as they don't lack important knowledge about the procedures or have false or unrealistic expectations of what their tattoo or piercing experience will be like. This is where you can help.

Think Before You Leap

You can help you teen think beyond the impulse of the moment by talking about the changing whims of fashion over the years. Like all fashion statements, piercings will probably fall out of style eventually. But unlike an out-of-style pair of baggy pants, body piercing can't be packed away. It becomes a permanent part of the body. Say to your teen:

"Before you get your body art, I just want you to think about it. Think about how your tastes naturally change with time and about how styles and trends also change. Decide if you'll still want this in ten years and won't be tired of the same old tattoo or piercing." (Then remind her of that Barbie wallpaper she wanted in her bedroom when she was seven.)

Your teen should also consider that what's New Age today is common tomorrow. You might observe, "It seems to me that an awful lot of adults and average kids are getting tattoos and piercings and turning an over-the-edge look into nerd ID." And what about ten years from now when the fad has passed? Today's teens may be branding themselves as the "older generation."

All of this may sound like an attempt to talk your teen out of the decision, but it's really just a way to help her think through ramifications that she may not be considering in her zeal for the latest style. If you don't at least help her think about these things, you can be sure that two years from now when she's tired of the look, you'll hear, "How could you let me do this?"

Your teen also needs to consider the whims of the workplace. Tattoos and piercings are not acceptable in certain jobs because they are perceived as unprofessional by most people. Tell your teen honestly:

"Although it's unfair to judge a person's work skills by his appearance, it does happen, and you should know that certain jobs and careers will be off-limits to you if you're tattooed or pierced."

Finally, make sure your teen understands the responsibility she'll take on for the proper care of the tattoo or piercing in the initial weeks following the procedure. Once she breaks through the skin, she needs consistent medical care that requires patience and effort.

If your teen is the kind of person who forgets to floss her teeth or clean her contact lenses, she should think twice before taking on the responsibility of caring for a tattoo or piercing.

Consider Alternatives
Before you or your teen commits to permanent body decorations, you might encourage him to look into noninvasive ways to "tattoo" and "pierce."

Temporary Tattoos. There are three kinds of temporary tattoos available that can give a person an idea of how the tattoo will look, where it is best positioned, and how he or she will feel about wearing it, and also give a sense of how important the tattoo is to self-image.

1. The most common kind is applied like a decal with water. It sells for a few dollars at most toy stores and lasts a day or two

before it washes or wears off. A local tattoo artist told us he'd tell his son to give this kind of temporary tattoo a try before he would let him get a permanent one. Most teens will not be thrilled with this option, however, which they might consider "kid stuff."

2. Another kind of temporary tattoo that is recently finding its way from Asian Indian culture to neighborhood tattoo parlors might be more appealing. It's called Indian *mehandi* (henna) tattooing. It looks and feels very real and lasts about a month. Henna tattoos are hand-painted on the skin (usually the hands or feet) with paste-like natural dyes that are then peeled off, revealing a beautiful, dark brown image. For about $20 to $40, your teen can have the experience of having a tattoo without the pain or the permanent skin damage.

3. Temporary tattoos applied with rice paper were used on Robert De Niro in *Cape Fear*, on Sean Penn at the end of *Dead Man Walking*, and on Bruce Willis's head in *12 Monkeys*. The process uses cosmetic ink printed on an archival cigarette-like tissue paper to paint in the "tattoo." The result is realistic and waterproof and lasts about two weeks.

As henna and rice paper tattooing come into the popular culture, many tattoo parlors are hiring artists trained in these techniques. If you're interested, use the yellow pages to call tattoo parlors near you or in the nearest metropolitan area; look for one that offers henna or rice paper tattoos.

Beware of the myth that you can get a temporary tattoo if the tattoo artist injects dye into the very shallow epidermal layer of the skin. There is no way to prevent the needles from entering the second layer (the dermis) of the skin.

Nonpierced Piercing. There are two types of body jewelry that your teen can purchase to try out the body-pierced look without actually putting holes in her body. The first type is a clip-on variety that works like the old clip-on earrings but is made specifically for the ear, nose, or lip. There are also magnetic rings that hold onto the "pierced" area by the force of magnets in the ring. Little New Age boutiques are often the best place to find these body rings.

TAKING THE PLUNGE

Once your teen knows the facts and then decides to go ahead with getting a tattoo or body piercing, don't step out of the picture. Although he may not want you to accompany him to get the job done, stick around to help him find a place where the procedure is done in a safe and clean environment. Tell him:

"I know you have a picture in your head of how good this is going to look, and I want that for you too. So I'm going to help you find a place where you can feel comfortable that the job won't be botched and you won't pick up any diseases."

Encourage your teen to call around or visit tattoo or piercing parlors, or offer to do the preliminary work yourself. When you contact an establishment, ask these questions:

- "What is the training of the person who gives the tattoos or piercings?"

   All tattooing and piercing should be performed by a professional—never by someone who is not specially trained.

Important nerve tissue, muscle tissue, and organs can suffer permanent injury in an improperly performed procedure.

- "Do you use a new needle for each customer? How is your equipment cleaned?"

It is also absolutely essential that the equipment be sterilized because it is possible to contract HIV, hepatitis, and other bloodborne diseases from an unsterilized needle during tattooing or body piercing. Equipment to sterilize, called an autoclave, should be standard in every tattooing or piercing studio. And a customer has the right to insist that the practitioner use a new needle on her. In some places this is standard practice; in others one must insist. Ask to see the needle package.

Tattooing and body piercing are in style right now. Next year the trend may be something more "shocking," more "daring," or perhaps more "normal." Who knows? But your role will stay the same. You have the right to investigate and to decide what you think is best for your teens. Whatever your decision, it's always best to talk about it, encourage dialogue about it, and make sure your teens know that you love them and care about them.

FOR FURTHER READING

Especially for Teens
Kauet, Herbert. *Coward's Guide to Body Piercing.* Boston: Boston America, 1996.

Reybold, Laura. *Everything You Need to Know About the Dangers of Tattooing and Body Piercing*. New York: Rosen Publishing Group, 1996.

Wilkinson, Beth. *Coping with the Dangers of Tattooing, Body Piercing, and Branding*. New York: Rosen Publishing Group, 1998.

Part Three

Concerns
of Teens

Competition

"I hate this team!" yelled fifteen-year-old Jane as she threw her spikes into the closet. "They're all awful—no wonder we never win. Nobody knows how to play. Nobody ever gives me the ball, so what's the point? I don't ever want to be seen with those losers again."

When Jane calmed down, her mother called her into the kitchen for a talk. There was a lot Jane needed to learn about the value of athletic competition beyond winning and losing.

Competition means comparing self with others, whether in athletics, in schoolwork, in the family, or in dance or piano competitions. In any arena, competition can spur one on to become the best one can be. Competition is an integral part of our society, a constant through all our years as we grow and compete for a spouse, for a job, for promotions, for recognition, for a place in the world. Our attitudes in these competitive situations and our ability to come out ahead are often molded by our experiences with competition during our growing years.

For many people, those experiences are gained on the athletic field. Here the goal is to get a good physical workout, learn the lessons of sportsmanship and about self-discipline and self-control. These things make it worthwhile to encourage teens to participate in sports at a time when many say they might prefer to get a job or hang out with friends.

For girls, there are additional reasons you might want to encourage athletic participation. The Women's Sports Foundation tells us that women who were active in sports as girls feel greater confidence, self-esteem, and pride in their physical and social selves than do those who were sedentary as kids. The foundation's research also suggests that girls who participate in sports are less likely to get involved with drugs, less likely to get pregnant, and more likely to graduate from high school than those who do not play sports. These are powerful reasons to stay involved in athletics.

To keep kids active and involved, you may need to sit down and talk to them about expectations, goals, and attitude. They need to know that sports are about more than just winning.

HOW TO TALK ABOUT COMPETITION

Competition is a subject you can best broach by talking first about *other* people. Use professional athletes as examples of good and bad sportsmanship. Talk about athletes' behavior and ask your kids what they would do in the same situation. The sports pages give you lots of stories to talk about. When basketball player Latrell Sprewell attacked his coach and was suspended for the season, there was a great debate over the severity of the punishment. When baseball player Roberto Alomar spit on an umpire, the press jumped all over the incident. These kinds of situations give you many opportunities to talk to your teens about the effects of sports beyond the final score.

You can also teach lessons about competition by talking to your kids about other players on their team or in their league. Never put down or criticize another player, but point out examples of good and bad behavior. If a talented player is very cocky and critical of others, you might simply say:

"It's too bad John feels the need to tell everyone how good he is. I think this attitude takes away from all the athletic skill he has. Being a good athlete never gives a person the right to ridicule or put down anyone else."

When you see a team "star" who leads her team with encouragement and support, point out this person to your teen and express admiration for that quality. Sports activities will give you many chances to talk about the good and bad aspects of competition.

When you talk to your teen about his or her own athletic performance, you should think before you speak:

• Whether your teen has won or lost the game, don't try to discuss the details of his performance while emotions are still running high. This is the time to follow his lead and give him time to settle down.

• Don't lecture. By the teen years, the coaches are in charge. If you insist on analyzing every play and every move your teen made, you will find yourself talking to deaf ears. Most teens now look to their coaches for advice.

• If you expect your teen to show good sportsmanship, make sure you do the same when you talk about the game. Don't put down other players. Don't criticize the referees. Don't make negative comments about the coaches. Say only what you would like your teens to repeat to others. This is how they learn how to be good sports, accept what happened without looking to blame others, learn something positive from the experience, and move on to prepare for the next game.

TALK ABOUT THE GOOD SIDE OF COMPETITION

By the time kids hit the high school level they've often lost sight of the benefits of competition beyond winning and losing. They compete only for the glory of winning and collapse in anger when they lose. Make sure they know that there are positive psychological and sociological reasons to participate in athletics as well. The Woman's Sports Foundation lists the following benefits your kids should know about:

- Stay healthy: physical activity strengthens the whole body, and a strong body can fight illness.
- Fight fat: one of the biggest reasons for fat is lack of exercise. Sports and exercise keep you trim and firm.
- Control anger and anxiety: exercise is nature's best tranquilizer; it actually helps keep you calm.
- Eat and sleep better: proper nutrition and rest improve every area of life.
- Learn to take criticism: this is a lesson we all need to learn in order to improve performance.
- Overcome shyness: learn to be assertive, make decisions.
- Learn how to be competitive yet cooperative by working together to attain goals.
- Learn how to deal with success as well as failure: self-esteem doesn't depend on continually winning.
- Learn responsibility: how to set goals and order priorities.

- Meet new friends; avoid boredom.
- Be able to talk to friends about sports—a popular topic of discussion and interest.

TALK ABOUT THE DOWNSIDE OF COMPETITION

Athletic competition has a lot going for it, but it also has a downside that you need to recognize and address. If you want your kids to have positive experiences through athletic activity, be sure to sit down and talk when you see any signs of the negative aspects of sports competition.

Kids Who Are Bad Losers

It's not uncommon to see an athlete throw down the equipment, swear at the opposing team, and kick the bench after losing a game. If your teen does this, it's up to you to step in and make sure she knows that this is unacceptable.

First, acknowledge that it's not fun to lose, but then let her know that her conduct is unsportsmanlike. Tell your teen:

"I know you're feeling angry and disappointed, but the way you act when you lose is unacceptable. If you want to continue to play, you have to learn to be a better sport. Learning how to lose is every bit as important as winning. At the next game you lose, I want to see you walk away quietly without throwing a tantrum. That will make me very proud of you."

Kids Who Burn Out

Throughout this century, psychologists have studied the risks of participation in organized sports programs. They have warned parents, coaches, and physical education teachers about the negative effects of overzealous competitions, of overly strenuous training, and of pressure to reach high expectations. All these things lead to what we now call sports burnout.

Sports burnout is not caused by sports participation. It is caused by the competitive environment and the win-at-all-costs attitude forced on young athletes by adults. It is caused when parents or coaches put too much pressure (consciously or unconsciously) on kids to become athletic stars. Some parents play out their own fantasies and dreams of glory—pushing the kids, interfering with the coaches and team, supporting obsessive hours of practice, often making huge financial sacrifices (even moving to be near a coach or in a better geographical region). The kids love it at first: being good at something, getting the attention, winning, being special. But they often burn out in the teen years, when they begin to be more independent in their thinking.

If from the beginning parents and coaches had put enjoyment of the sport, the learning of skills, teamwork with friends, and good sportsmanship above winning and excelling as the star, many more young athletes would stay in sports programs and would still be active ten, twenty, even thirty years down the line.

Some athletes are more prone to burnout than others. Highly susceptible athletes are often accomplished performers who strive to meet high, sometimes unrealistic, goals. They tend to invest a great deal of time and effort trying to meet these goals. They usually don't react well to criticism; they may have a weak support system and will often suffer from boredom if the training regime is too repetitious.

There are signs of sports burnout that will give you an indication that it's time to look at your young athlete's training regimen

and your own attitude, which may be contributing to athletic stress
and pressure. You should look for

Lack of self-esteem
Anxiety
Depression
Fatigue
Insomnia
Withdrawal
Declining athletic performance
Chronic injuries
Cynical and critical attitude toward the sport

Dr. David Feigley, director of the Youth Research Council at
Rutgers University in New Jersey, has studied sports attrition, and
he cautions that burnout shouldn't be confused with dropout. He
says that kids drop out of sports for many rather common reasons.
Some drop out of one sport but pick up another. Some drop out to
move on to other things. (This is especially prevalent in the teenage
years, when young people have more independent mobility and
more options about how to use their time.) Some drop out because
their priorities have changed—maybe now they want to spend more
time with friends or work to save money for college.

Burnout, says Dr. Feigley, is different—it is specifically related
to stress. Young athletes burn out when they are emotionally
exhausted and get trapped in a situation where they feel out of control. To put it simply, the teen has overdosed. The kids who are
training five days a week, twelve months a year can get to a point
where they just don't want to do it—period. Between the ages of
thirteen and fifteen, when kids start to reason more like adults, they
often decide they've had enough.

Burnout seems to happen most often with the kids who care about their sport the most. It happens especially in sports that require year-round, rigorous training. This includes (but is certainly not limited to) sports like gymnastics, tennis, skating, and swimming. It happens to athletes who have coaches or parents who set unrealistic goals.

Dr. Feigley has a few suggestions that might assist you in helping your teen avoid burnout:

- Look for ways to give your kids some autonomy. Let them set their practice schedule when possible. Let them pick a day of the week when they can skip a practice if they choose. Let them feel some control over whether they want to do this activity or not. It makes the reason for being at practice (even just one practice) a self-motivated reason.

- Allow more flexibility in the practice schedule. Teens resent the time they put into their sport when it starts to interfere with other important areas of their life. They need to be able occasionally to shorten, skip, or move a practice when they need to study, when their friends are all going to a school function, or when Grandma is visiting from out of town. This reduces the feeling of being trapped in something with no way out.

- Give them a break. High-level, year-round athletes need a break in their training to stay strong and focused. Athletes need at least several weeks a year to rest and recover and to come back physically and psychologically strong. If your athlete is showing signs of burnout, ask her if she would like to take a break during the off-season. Knowing there is an end in sight may give her what she needs to hold on.

- Try cross-training. Letting kids play different sports often revives interest in their primary sport and keeps them physically fit.

This may be a difficult solution, because the day of the three-letter athlete is quickly passing. For kids to compete on the upper levels, coaches today often insist on exclusivity; they don't want their athletes playing other sports, even during off-season. But talk to your kid's coach and find out if this is a possible solution to your teen's burnout problem.

- Work on time management. Kids who excel in their sport usually also excel in other areas as well and are not very good at saying no. They are class officers, club members, student leaders, church members, and so on. Help your kids schedule their events to create some free time so that there is not so much stress and conflict. Maybe they can choose a few activities to give less time to. Maybe they can step down as the president or captain of some groups. Maybe they can agree to stop adding more responsibilities to their day.

- Be involved with your child's school. Choosing teachers who are organized and able to work with your child's athletic schedule can greatly reduce the pressure of trying to excel in athletics and academics. Talk to your child's guidance counselor in early spring, when the following year's schedule is being put together; work together to create a schedule that will help reduce stress. Can she pick her teachers? Can she take a study hall? Can she take her most important and difficult classes in the middle of the day, so she won't miss them if she has to leave early for a meet or if she is tired in the morning after a late-night competition? Can she get credit through some kind of gifted-and-talented program for the time dedicated to a high-level sport? Check out these possibilities. They can make a big difference.

Kids Who Get Overly Frustrated When They Lose

If your kids see winning as the be-all and end-all of playing sports, you will often end up with an unhappy, frustrated child. If your teen gets overly upset after a loss, it might be because of his competitive style. Sports psychologists tell us that all kids have one of two competitive styles. The *outcome-oriented* style can lead to a lot of frustration. Kids who have adopted this style make judgments about themselves based on outcomes: "If I win, I'm good," they reason. "If I lose, I'm not good." This makes losing very frustrating, especially when they believe that they're worthy of love only if they win. You'll hear complaints like these: "I stink." "I'm not good at anything." "I shouldn't even be playing with this team."

If this sounds like your teen, you can try to bring her over to the *performance-oriented* competitive style. Competitors who have adopted this style assume they're good enough to excel eventually, and they judge themselves by personal improvement gains: "I lost the match today, but I didn't double fault like last week."

The difference between these two competitive styles is the difference between a teen's saying, "I'm proud of who I beat and where I rank," and his saying, "I'm proud of what I did." The difference may seem insignificant, but it speaks volumes about attitude. If you're only proud about having beaten someone, you'll feel humiliated when you go from the junior varsity to the varsity and—although your skills have improved—fall behind in rank. Going from the top of the beginners to the bottom of the advanced causes many kids to quit in embarrassment and frustration. The twelve-year-old phenom who moves up a division with everyone expecting him to be an instant winner will beat himself up mentally when the physically older and stronger teammates steal the spotlight. This is because he's making judgments about his self-worth based on his rank rather than his accomplishments.

Try the following dialogues to promote the performance-oriented style of competition in your teens:

- Take the focus off being the best player. Instead, stress the importance of doing one's personal best and showing good sportsmanship. Say, "Losing can be very frustrating, but even in the games you lose, you learn something that will help you do better in the next game."

- Find something to cheer about. Praise effort and attitude. Say, "I'm glad to see you didn't hang your head when you missed that point. You gave it your best shot, and that's what counts."

- Avoid asking, "Did you win?" Instead, focus on personal achievement. Ask: "How did you play today?"

- Be alert to signs of too much stress: losing equipment, chronic lateness to events, illness the day of games.

- Help them develop a resilience that allows them to evaluate their efforts as separate from themselves. Say, "You may have struck out, but I still love you."

- Help them build self-improvement goals into their practice sessions. Say things like: "Can you put more backhands into the left side of the court?" "Can you improve your free-throw shooting from 70 to 75 percent?" "Can you cut your time down by 1 percent?" Kids who set personal goals can see accomplishments regardless of their ranking. Practices become more fun.

- Help them feel OK whether they win or lose so that they do not confuse performance with self-worth. Say, "Let's go get a burger to celebrate what a good kid you are."

Kids Who Are Afraid to Compete

Fear of making mistakes and of being humiliated keeps many kids off athletic playing fields. (This is especially puzzling when it happens to a teen who had been very active in sports in earlier grades.)

If your teen seems afraid to compete, consider that there are several possible reasons for this fear:

> It may be caused by the development of perfectionist tendencies that cause people to stay away from things they can't do perfectly.
>
> It may be caused by the teenager's newly developed obsession with appearing cool at all times.
>
> It may be caused by evolving insecurities that push teens behind the scenes for a while until they get a better grasp of who they are.
>
> It may happen when a former "star" is humiliated by the fact that teammates have caught up in size and ability and he or she no longer shines.

Whatever the cause, the fear of failing is very real, and you should take some time to help your teen overcome this obstacle. Ironically, it's failure that teaches the most valuable lessons about success. That's why it's important that our teens learn that failures are an inevitable and useful part of life.

Talk About Failure. When your teens talk about their failures and mistakes in everyday activities, listen for a tendency to blame others or to give up too quickly. If your children aren't doing well in school, do they blame the teacher or say, "What's the use"? If their school project turns out awful, do they blame the materials or give up in anger? If they lose the game, do they blame their teammates or decide they're just no good? If your kids are reacting like this, they may believe that failing at one or two things makes them a total failure. Perfectionists, especially, feel that their self-worth depends on external factors, such as being successful at everything they do. These teens need to learn about the positive side of failure.

Mistakes are a positive part of everyone's daily life, so it's not difficult to find opportunities to talk about this subject:

- When your teen brings home a school paper with a mistake, for example, don't focus on the grade alone; talk about the error. Say, "Making mistakes is one of the ways we learn things. So let's see what you can learn from this mistake." Then help your child find the correct answer.
- If your child tries to put together a project and it falls apart before it's finished, encourage him or her to use this event constructively. Ask, "Why do you think it fell apart?" "What can you do differently the next time?" "Let's see you give it another try."

Talk About Your Own Failures. You can encourage your kids to risk failure by talking about your own experience with risk taking and by admitting your mistakes and failures. You might talk to your kids about the time you ran for class president and lost, or tried out for a team and didn't make it, or tried to build a model airplane by yourself but found that you needed help. These admissions give your teen permission to fail also.

Help Your Children Practice Failure. Everyone needs to learn and accept that no one can be the best at everything, that no one can win all the time, and that it's possible to enjoy a game even when you don't win. In short, it's human to fail and make mistakes, and this imperfection does not diminish our self-worth or reduce our chances of succeeding in the future.

One way to teach this lesson is to arrange situations in which you occasionally let your teens fail. If you play card or board games, for example, don't always let your kids win. If you play tennis or basketball, don't consistently give them the advantage. Let them experience the disappointment of losing in a protected environment. Then encourage them to try again. It's these little lessons that give our children the confidence and perseverance they'll need to master difficult tasks and pursue challenging goals in their lives.

When your teen takes even a small step forward in dealing with his or her fear of competing, be sure to comment. Bring attention to the fact that it's the effort, far more than the outcome, that matters most. You might say, "I think your backhand was much stronger today." Or, "You're getting much better at thinking ahead before you move your chess pieces." These words of encouragement applaud effort and improvement no matter what the overall outcome of a game.

If your teen will not join a sports team and you believe it's because of fear, you might try to refocus the goal. Encourage your teens to try an individual sport (such as track, swimming, tennis, bowling, gymnastics) where he or she can focus on self-improvement rather than team success. These sports give many people opportunities to compete, stay fit, and learn new skills, without the pressure sometimes associated with team sports.

Kids Who Take Performance-Enhancing Drugs

Performance-enhancing drugs are not in themselves bad or dangerous. They are a group of powerful synthetic substances, called anabolic steroids, that resemble the male sex hormone, testosterone, which is produced naturally in the male's testes. The drugs are legally prescribed for treatment of certain types of diseases and ailments.

Steroids become injurious to health and even deadly when they are used nonmedically and illegally to enhance body size and athletic performance. The exact number of athletes who abuse steroids is unknown because nonmedical use is illegal, and therefore no one publicizes its use. However, as college, professional, and Olympic teams begin to require steroid testing before competitions, the large number of athletes involved in steroid use is beginning to come to light. As steroid use by athletic role models and sports idols continues to make headlines, it becomes easy to see that the use of these drugs is no longer confined to dingy, smelly gyms where obsessive body builders secretively load up in dark corners. Steroid abuse has crept into all U.S. sports and is openly practiced in posh health spas, fitness centers, local gymnasiums, and even high school locker rooms. In fact, a survey found that 6.6 percent of male high school seniors have used steroids and that 40 percent of these boys began using the drugs before they reached the age of sixteen.

Why would talented young athletes, many of whom would never think of abusing alcohol, cocaine, or marijuana, take steroids? A piece of the complex answer lies in the nature of sports competition. In overly competitive environments, athletes are sometimes tempted to alter their physical makeup and size to improve their performance, impress their peers, please their coaches and parents, and make them better than their opponents (or merely equal, if they believe their opponents are taking the drugs). They see only the positive effects: a sense of euphoria, an aggressive and vigorous attitude, larger muscle size in less training time, and increased amounts of energy and speed.

What teens don't immediately see are the negative body changes that steroid abuse can cause. That's why they need to hear from you that you know about the temptation of steroids but that they are just too dangerous. Tell them what their friends won't: that

as soon as the user stops taking the drugs, the extra weight and muscle mass are quickly lost, but many of the negative effects stay
behind. Tell your teen about these negative side effects (selected
from a long list):

> *Psychological problems* include mood depression, nervous ten-
> sion, irritability, hostility, aggression, sleep problems, delu-
> sions, and even suicidal tendencies.
> *Physical problems* include acne, breast development in males,
> cancer of the liver, decreased sperm count, heart disease,
> hairiness in women, baldness in women, oily skin and hair,
> stunted growth, and sterility.

Talk to your teens about these two other aspects of steroid use
that affect them:

> *Career issues.* Tell your teens, "College teams don't want
> athletes if their athletic performance is the result of 'juice'
> rather than natural ability." (And they do test their athletes
> for steroid use.)
> *Ethical issues.* Tell your teens, "Steroid use is cheating—cheat-
> ing in the sport, cheating fellow athletes, and cheating one's
> own body."

The use of steroids is a serious issue that tends to get swept
under the carpet in any discussion of athletic performance. Bring it
out in the open and make sure your young athletes know that
because you love them, you will insist on a blood test the minute
you suspect that anything other than hard work and effort is behind
their muscle growth and physical performance.

THINK ABOUT YOUR ROLE

You have to take a good look at yourself and your feelings about sports if you expect to influence your teens' ideas about athletic competition. What you say and do at their sporting events says much more to your kids than what you say during quiet conversations. You should promise yourself that you will abide by the following unofficial code of conduct for parents drawn up by the National Association for Sport and Physical Education (NASPE). These are commonsense guidelines, but some parents need the reminder:

- Remain seated in the spectator area during the game.
- Don't yell instructions or criticism at the athletes.
- Refrain from making derogatory comments to players or parents of the opposing team, to officials, or to league administrators.
- Do nothing that will detract from the enjoyment your child gets from the sport.

It's not a secret that some parents push too hard. They make every moment of their kids' lives a competitive and action-packed quest to be *the best*. This sets kids up for their own perfectionistic difficulties, where losing is tragic and winning is all that counts. Have an honest talk with yourself and ask, "Just whose desires are being filled when my child competes?" If your teen is competing to please you, neither of you will end up happy or satisfied.

Don't let your own need for a high-achieving athlete push your child to perform. Encourage him to look inside himself to find his own motivation and desire for success. Then back off and see what happens.

TALK ABOUT THE LESSONS OF LOSING

No matter how many times you emphasize the positive, your teens will still feel disappointed when they lose an athletic event. That's OK—losing is part of life. H. J. Saunders of the Youth Fitness Coalition advises parents to say, "Nobody likes losing, but we've all got to deal with it. Acknowledge the negative and move on. Just because you lost the game, it doesn't mean you're a loser in life. In fact, we get stronger every time we bounce back."

All teen athletes need to know that the winners in life are not only those who come out number one. Winners are not just those who win—they are those who by competing come out with self-discipline and self-esteem, those who can face a challenge, take a risk, accept responsibility, and persevere to overcome obstacles. These are the rewards of competition—win or lose.

Although sport programs for teenagers often do put more emphasis on winning and on team and individual records than youth leagues do (or should), that doesn't take away the underlying reason for participating in high school sports. Only a tiny fraction of high school athletes go on to college athletics, and only a minuscule fraction of those go on to professional athletics—it makes sense to help your teen focus on more than winning.

FOR FURTHER READING

Murphy, Shane. *The Cheers and the Tears: A Positive Alternative to the Dark Side of Youth Sports*. San Francisco: Jossey-Bass, 1999.

Cults

The article about eternal salvation for teens caught the eye of fifteen-year-old Joanne, who was involved in her church's teen Bible-study group. Joanne sent away for a free subscription and soon was receiving reams of information that gave her newfound confidence and insightful ideas that impressed her peers. Even her family was pleased with her interest in the life of Jesus Christ.

But what had started out as an innocent curiosity soon became an obsession. Joanne began to spend more time studying the Bible, avoiding friends and family. Her attitude also began to change. She acted like she knew a secret no one else would understand. When asked about it, she was evasive, explaining that "only those who are called" can comprehend the truth.

Joanne graduated from high school and went off to college. There two "elders" came to visit her, encouraging her to attend their services and offering her a ride. Soon Joanne was hooked. She changed her manner of dress and her diet. She prayed, fasted, and meditated over the cult literature. She agreed to give up her social life outside the group, cease her "worldly" activities, and donate her spare time to raise money for the church. She also agreed to forsake her mother and father and anyone else outside the cult.

This all happened so gradually and so innocently that Joanne's family was not fully aware of the cult influence on their daughter's life until she informed them that she would never see them again. By then it was too late. The cult indoctrination was so deep, no amount of talking or pleading could change Joanne's mind.

This is a very typical story of cult involvement. What is most frightening about these groups is that teens and young adults are the major target of cult recruiters. When Michael Langone, Ph.D. (editor of *Cultic Studies Journal* and executive director of America's Family Foundation), surveyed 308 former members of 101 different cults, he found that 43 percent of them were recruited as students: 10 percent were high school students, 27 percent were college undergraduates, and 6 percent were graduate students. Of this group, 38 percent dropped out of school after joining the cult. Cult recruiters know that young people are especially vulnerable to cult influence because they are questioning the world and making changes in their lives. Cults and their recruiting tactics are subjects that all teens need to know about.

CULTS IN AMERICA

The most renown and infamous cults—the Heaven's Gate extraterrestrial cult (which in 1997 ordered the mass suicide of thirty-nine of its members), the People's Temple group led by Jim Jones (which staged the notorious "Kool-Aid" mass murder–suicides), and David Koresh's Branch Davidians (who met a fiery death in Waco, Texas)—grab headlines and shock us with their macabre nature. Are these people kooks? Weirdos? Gullible? Stupid? What would make a sane person join a cult?

The truth is that cults are not a rarity, and their members do not usually appear any different from you or me. Dr. Langone gives a conservative estimate that there are approximately five thousand different cults in the United States today, which claim as many as two to three million members. There are neo-Christian religious cults; Hindu and Eastern religious cults; occult, witchcraft, and satanic cults; mystical cults; Zen and other Sino-Japanese philosophical-mystical cults; racial cults; flying saucer and outer-space cults; psychological or psychotherapeutic cults; political cults; and self-help, self-improvement, and lifestyle systems cults. (Many cults fall into multiple categories.) And experts suspect that the number of cults will swell as we enter the new millennium.

HOW TEENS GET HOOKED ON CULTS

How do cults get sane, intelligent young people to turn away from those they love and join their group? Surprisingly, cult methods of recruiting and indoctrinating are not exotic forms of mind control. They use well-known methods of social influence—but in extreme doses.

Your teen will not join a "cult." He or she will join an interesting group of people who promise eternal happiness. The members will offer instant friendship, respect for contributions, an identity, safety, and an organized daily schedule. The group will offer to mend any gaping holes in the teen's life.

The holes in teens' lives can be caused by any of many life situations: a new home, a new school, divorcing parents, or a romantic breakup. These holes are especially difficult to bear for children who find school trivial, who have little social life, who live in broken families. Cults promise to make the world right again. They offer a simple route to happiness: "Follow me," cult leaders proclaim. "I know the path to happiness, peace, security, and salvation."

The problem with this "solution" is that the offer is only temporary. It is a manipulative technique employed to get vulnerable people to join. When they do, they get trapped in a powerful and persuasive environment that restricts their choices so that they can no longer evaluate the reality of their situation. Outsiders can see that the group is a bad influence, but the new recruit can't.

All people, but especially teens who are naturally emotionally vulnerable, need certain things to feel whole and fulfilled. Cults know what these things are, and they offer them in bountiful quantity. These things include the following:

A sense of community and a feeling of commonly shared goals and ideas

A need for inner fulfillment and the direct experience of spiritual values

A sense of meaning in life and a purpose for living

A strong, external structure that encourages separation in individuals who are overly dependent on their parents

The very things that attract young people to cults give us our first clue about how to keep kids out of cults.

KEEPING KIDS OUT OF CULTS

Cults are a phenomenon we will always have with us, both the large, well-organized groups and the smaller groups that seem to be popping up on every street corner. They exist as part of the frayed edges of our society and are not going away. But they do have vital messages that we can learn from and use to protect our children. Prevention is the emphasis here. Talking to your teenagers in a consistently open and loving manner will give them the emotional armor they need to resist the allure of cults.

The premise of this book is that families who talk about important issues are families that build a strong and loving bond. It is unlikely that this kind of bond will be broken by a fast-talking cult recruiter.

Give your children what the cults promise:

Unconditional Love. Tell your teenagers daily, "I love you." Even withdrawn, sulky, and belligerent teens need to hear this every day.

Acceptance. When your teen experiments with some outlandish style in clothes or music, don't criticize. Simply say something like, "I don't personally like that look, but underneath it I know there's one great kid."

Understanding. When you disagree, don't always fight so hard to prove you're right. Instead, try: "I don't agree with you, but tell me more, because I want to understand your point of view."

Concern. When you see your teenager is sad or sulky, don't ignore it, hoping it will pass. Show your concern with kind words.

Say, "You look down. Is there anything I can do? Would you like to talk? I have plenty of time to listen. If you need anything, you know you can come to me."

These are the same questions a cult recruiter will ask a depressed teenager. Make sure your teen hears these words first at home.

Spirituality. There's an old saying that explains why it's important to give your teenagers a spiritual base to work from: "If you don't stand for something, you'll fall for anything." A spiritual base doesn't necessarily have to be built in a church or synagogue, but if you are confused about morality issues, spiritual values, and the meaning of life, your children may be more easily swayed by a kind cult leader who tells teens they live in a cold, cruel world where no one cares about them.

For this reason, make sure your teen knows what you believe in and sees you put it into action. Use daily experiences to talk about your beliefs:

• If there is a news story that focuses on a question of honesty, give your opinion on it: "I believe honesty is vital to a trusting relationship. That's why I will always be honest with you and hope you will be with me."

• If you do a charitable deed, let everyone in your house know about it: "Pick out any old clothes you have and put them in the den. I'm donating them to the local clothing drive."

• If you notice a random act of kindness, point it out and talk about it: "Did you see that man help that elderly woman put her grocery packages in the car? It's so nice to see that some people really care about strangers."

Show your kids that you stand for something so that they will be less likely to fall for cult promises.

FOREWARN AND FOREARM

Cult participation is just one more subject we can't ignore with fingers crossed hoping our teenagers won't be victimized. It's another subject that has to be brought out in the open and talked about (ideally) before there is any danger. If teens are forearmed with facts, they will be in a better position to resist the coercive and deceptive techniques of the cults. Discuss the following issues with your teens in casual conversations that allow them to be naturally inquisitive and to ask questions:

The Basic Beliefs

Introduce the existence of cults with the renowned and infamous examples of Heaven's Gate and Jim Jones's People's Temple. Further explain that smaller, less well known cults also exist in ordinary neighborhoods. Make sure your teens know the facts:

- A cult is a group that violates the rights of its members, harms them through abusive techniques of mind control, and distinguishes itself from a normal social or religious group by subjecting its members to physical, mental, or financial deprivation or deception to keep them in the group.
- Cult members band together under a charismatic leader.
- They use deceptive tactics in their indoctrination process, including trance induction, prolonged chanting, detailed interrogations, long lectures, long sermons, or exhausting work routines, in order to suppress doubts and enforce compliance.

- Most cults want their members to give money, work for free, beg, and recruit new members.
- The danger of cults lies in a mindless devotion that severs ties with family and friends, creates total dependence on the group for identity, and imposes high exit costs by creating phobias of harm, failure, and personal isolation.

Recruitment Tactics

Recruitment is no longer practiced only in airports and on street corners. Recruiters are in schools, at sports events, at video hangouts, in magazines, and on the World Wide Web. They zero in on teens who appear lonely or sad. They strike up conversations that show great concern and love. They make arrangements to meet again sometime. The process usually takes place slowly, over a period of time. When the recruiter has gained the trust and confidence of the teen, then the teen is invited to a "meeting."

Critical thinking skills can be used as solid defense weapons against cult recruiters. The American Family Foundation gives young people the following list to help them recognize common cult recruitment tactics and situations. In casual conversations and during teachable moments, warn your kids to be wary of the following:

- People who are excessively or inappropriately friendly. Genuine friendships take time to build.
- People with simplistic answers or solutions to complex world problems.
- People with invitations to free meals, lectures, and workshops.
- People who pressure you to do something you don't really want to do. Don't be afraid to say no.
- People who are vague or evasive. If they are hiding something, it's usually because they don't want you to know!

- People who try to play on your basic human decency. You don't always have to reciprocate a kindness, for example, especially when it may have been given as a way to manipulate you.
- People who claim to be "just like you." This is often a device for disarming your vigilance.
- People who confidently claim that they can help you solve your problems, especially when they know little about you.
- People who make grand claims about saving humankind, achieving enlightenment, or following the road to happiness. If their claims seem too good to be true, they are probably false!
- People who always seem "happy," even when common sense would dictate otherwise.
- People who claim they or their group is "really special." Arrogance is much more common than genuine superiority.
- People who claim that "you need to destroy the mind to find God" or that "the devil works thorough the mind," or who otherwise disparage the critical mind. Your mind is your primary defense against psychological manipulation. Protect it!

Discuss the Concept of Religion

Although not all cults are based on religions, many are, so it is important to talk to your teens about the differences between cults and traditional religions. You might emphasize that traditional religions look up to a supreme being for direction and grace. They work together for the good of society and the hope of eternal life. They are open to all. They encourage potential members to think carefully before making a commitment to join. They do not encourage members to disown their families.

Most cults, in contrast, look up to a charismatic human leader who operates in an authoritarian manner and who inspires blind (often sexual) devotion. Members give their money, their affection, and their allegiance to this person, who strips members of their identity and their families.

Indoctrination Techniques

Cult leaders are very good at mind control. They skillfully take away a person's free will and self-esteem. The specific techniques used by cults to ensnare and control the minds of their members are many and varied, but for general discussion, you can tell your teen that cults often use the following indoctrination techniques:

Initial misrepresentation about the name of the group and its purposes

Isolation from family and friends

Sleep deprivation

Protein-deficient diets (high in sugar and starch)

Exotic rituals that raise group emotions to intense peaks

Physical exertion and fatigue to narrow consciousness and the ability to think independently

"Love-bombing"—that is, responding to one's emotional and social needs by showering one with attention, love, peer support, and approval

Lack of privacy

Continuous supervision in a completely controlled environment where no contrary information is allowed

One of the most effective prevention tactics against indoctrination is to allow the growth of a strong, independent mind. Encourage autonomy and independent thinking in your teens by giving them opportunities to make their own decisions. Let them choose their own friends, select their own clothes, and enjoy their own music. The more they are able to think for themselves, the less likely they will be to depend on cult leaders for direction in their lives.

WHAT'S THE BIG DEAL?

At first, your teens may not understand why cults are a big deal. They may figure that if somebody wants to join a new group of friends who makes him feel good, why not? This is the point of your discussion. Your teens need to know that cults are destructive in many ways. Any one of the following is a good reason to stay away from cults. Let your teen know that cults

Use unethical and manipulative techniques to recruit and hold members

Arouse high levels of guilt and anxiety

Induce trancelike states that can impair judgment and heighten suggestibility

Cause radical personality changes in members, which inhibit normal psychological and social development

Destroy family relationships

Inflict physical, psychological, and financial damage on members

Encourage unlawful and antisocial values and behaviors

Do not allow members to express doubts or question given "truths"

Hold a paranoid view of the outside world as evil

Impose intense group pressure to conform

Cult membership is a very big deal. Most members stay with the cult for an average of five years—that's a very long time to be isolated from family and friends. And many who leave take with them psychological scars that last a lifetime.

WHAT TO DO IF YOUR TEEN IS RECRUITED INTO A CULT

If you suspect your teenager has already joined a cult, look for the typical symptoms that experts tell us are almost always present in cult members. The following are the first significant warning signals:

- Change of lifestyle
- Change of goal
- Separation from family and friends
- Sudden demarcation between all that is good and right on the cult side and all that is bad on the other.

Stay Calm

You must remain calm, logical, and patient (a hard thing to do when you're feeling desperate about your child's welfare). Anger and hysteria only confirm their fears, serving to drive teenagers further into involvement.

- Do not attack the group. Avoid name calling and emphasis on the word *cult*. This approach can be counterproductive if your child is just beginning to be swayed by the group's propaganda, which can include impressive, high-sounding philosophies and goals.

- Remain open minded and avoid rigid positions. Views that may sound heretical are not necessarily destructive. Focus instead on the restriction of free choice through manipulation and deception.

- Discuss the situation in a sincere, respectful, nonjudgmental, and consistent manner. If you cry or attack, your teen will shut down, and you'll have no chance of opening her eyes.

Ask Questions

Before quizzing your teen, find out as much as you can about the group so that you can discuss it intelligently. See if you can get the group's own literature to learn from. Call the American Family Foundation (listed at the end of the chapter); they have information on some specific groups.

When you're ready to talk to your teen, ask questions calmly and with genuine interest. Ask:

"Do they have meetings open to the public so that I might attend?" (Cult meetings are *always* closed.)

"Have they told you that your parents wouldn't understand the truths they profess?"

"Do they claim to love you more than your family does?"

"Have they forewarned you that your family will call the group a cult?"

"Have you been told to take your time, consider all the alternatives, and consult with those whose judgment you trust?" (You may not get an honest answer to this question, but it might make your teen think about the way he is being pushed to commit so quickly.)

Don't Argue

You won't convince your teen that this newfound group of friends
is evil. But the answers to the preceding questions will do two
things: (1) they will give you the information you need to decide if
your teen has been recruited by a cult, and (2) if it is early in the
indoctrination process, they may give your teen a reason to question further involvement.

Get Help

If your teen is a participating member of a cult engaging in mind
control, you will need professional help to bring him out of the grasp
of the cult. He needs a therapist who is specially trained in the
process of mind control and brainwashing and who has knowledge
of the specific content of the group to which the teen belongs, so as
to identify the language system, buzzwords, philosophical teachings,
the specific types of behavioral control used, and the demands to
which the teen has been subjected.

If your teen leaves home and is totally in the grip of a cult, you
might consider a process called deprogramming. Deprogrammers are
agents of force hired by parents to rescue their children. The depro-
grammer will "kidnap" the teen and isolate him or her in order to
deprogram the effects of brainwashing. This is a very controversial
method and has landed many families in court on legal charges, but
it is an option.

Once a teen returns home, family discussions are no longer
an equal match for the psychological tactics used by the cult.
Get professional help by calling the American Family Foundation. They will refer you to a therapist in your area trained in exit
counseling.

RESOURCES

American Family Foundation (AFF)
P.O. Box 2265
Bonita Springs, FL 34133
(914) 533-5420
Web site: http://www.csj.org

The AFF is a professional research and educational organization founded in 1979 to assist cult victims and their families through the study of cults and psychological manipulation. The Web site contains resource listings, links to other organizations, a group index of AFF's *Cult Observer*, abstracts from AFF's *Cultic Studies Journal*, and other practical information.

FOR FURTHER READING

Especially for Teens
Barden, Renardo. *Cults*. Vero Beach, Fla.: Rourke, 1990.

Cohen, Daniel. *Cults*. Highland Park, N.J.: Mill Brook Press, 1994.

Porterfield, Kay Marie. *Straight Talk About Cults*. New York: Facts on File, 1997.

Depression

Jennifer was usually quick to jump into a fight with her dad. He braced for the attack when he announced that she had to be back in the house by ten o'clock. But this time Jennifer surprised him. "OK," she sighed. "I don't really care." On the one hand, Jennifer's dad was relieved that there would be no shouting match tonight, but on the other hand, he was concerned. Jennifer had been acting very sad and quiet lately. She sat around her room all weekend, hadn't eaten much in a couple of days, and even gave her little sister her prized CD collection. And now came this reaction, which wasn't at all like her. When Jennifer's dad asked what was the matter, Jennifer said, "Nothing." What can you say after that?

Everyone gets depressed at some time. Feeling low or blue is a normal reaction to the stresses of everyday life; it is as normal as feeling happy or hopeful. But your teens may not have the life experiences they need to know that feeling depressed is not the end of the world. Talking about these feelings, even when your teens say nothing is wrong, is the first step in helping teens deal with depression before the pain pushes them to thoughts of suicide.

WHEN TO TALK ABOUT DEPRESSION

Typically, depression is triggered in the teen years by an upsetting experience: the death of a grandparent, the divorce of parents, a move to a new city or school, the breakup of a relationship, or even the loss of an important athletic competition. These kinds of experiences should alert you to be on the lookout for signs of depression, which can include the following:

Persistent sad, anxious, or "empty" mood
Feelings of hopelessness, pessimism
Feelings of guilt, worthlessness, helplessness
Loss of interest or pleasure in ordinary activities
Sleep disturbances (insomnia, early morning waking, or over-
    sleeping)
Eating disturbances (loss of appetite and weight, or weight gain)
Decreased energy, fatigue, being "slowed down"
Restlessness, irritability
Difficulty concentrating, remembering, and making decisions

At times, depressive disorders can masquerade as persistent physical symptoms that do not respond to treatment, such as headaches, chest or stomach pains, fatigue, dizziness, digestive disorders, and chronic pain.

There are also some signs of depression that are more typical in one gender than the other. Depressed boys often react to the pain of depression by breaking off friendships, ceasing to care about schoolwork, or cursing the world. Depressed teenage girls often punish themselves by bingeing on food, starving themselves, or verbally lamenting their faults and failures. These are all cries for help that shouldn't be ignored.

HOW TO TALK ABOUT DEPRESSION

When you see your teen in the grip of depression, you might think it's best to respect his privacy and wait quietly for the blues to pass. But if the symptoms of depression are obvious to you, it's a good bet that your teen is waiting for you to say something to show you've noticed and care about his pain.

When you bring up the subject, keep these tips in mind:

Take the Initiative. A depressed teen may want to talk but not know how to begin. Don't be afraid to be direct: "I've noticed that you seem withdrawn [angry, sad, or whatever] lately. Let's talk about it."
Or, simply ask: "Are you happy?"

Offer Sympathy (Not Solutions). If your teen opens up to you, don't jump in with a quick solution; just let him know you understand: "Sometimes moving to a new school can be so difficult. I understand why you feel like you'll never be happy again."

Respect Painful Feelings. Your teen's emotions are important to him. Even if they seem trivial to you, take them seriously and spend time helping him sort them out: "This must really hurt you. Do you think you're more sad or angry about this?"

Offer Empathy. Offer a story from your own life that will show your teen not only that you understand his pain but also that the pain passes and life goes on.

Brainstorm (Don't Dictate) Solutions. You can help your teen learn how to cope with depression by helping him think about ways to help himself. You might suggest that he lower his expectations (especially if he's a perfectionist); change some things in his schedule or environment; spend more time with friends; spend more time in some physical activity; organize an outing as a diversion. Encourage your teen to brainstorm with you, reminding him that he doesn't have to do all the things you think of; just throw out many ideas hoping to come up with one or two good ones.

If you listen intently, show your support, and help your teen think of ways to cope and regain some personal control, the depression may resolve itself. In most cases, depressed moods last only a few hours or a few days and are valuable learning experiences. We all need to learn that sadness is as much a part of life as happiness. But if the mood doesn't pass, then it's possible that your child may be experiencing a deep, despairing depression called clinical depression.

RECOGNIZING CLINICAL DEPRESSION

The feelings of despair in clinical depression are far deeper and more destructive than feelings that accompany the more common bouts of depression we all experience. Although this kind of depression can also be triggered by an upsetting experience, profound feelings of worthlessness and lack of self-esteem often underlie the obvious cause.

If some or all of the symptoms of depression persist for more than two weeks or are causing impairment in ordinary functioning, then your teen needs professional help. Don't hesitate to reach out—depression is a complex disorder with many causes. If your teen is depressed, it doesn't mean you're a bad parent; it doesn't mean he is emotionally weak. It means he is having trouble dealing with one of the many emotions of life. He may also be showing an inherited tendency that makes him more sensitive to life's upsets. Whatever the cause, don't ignore the early signs of clinical depression. Sadly, severe depression, if left untreated, in teens too often leads to suicide.

SUICIDE

Devastating depression is the major reason people kill themselves. Feeling lonely and engulfed by sadness, they do not know how to reach out to others or find relief from the pain that plagues them. At this point, some begin to see death as their only way out.

This does not mean that every depressed person commits, attempts, or even thinks about suicide, nor that every suicide comes about as a result of depression. But a large number of suicides and suicide attempts among young people can be linked to a state of severe depression.

Globally, some five hundred thousand teenagers attempt suicide every year. That means that every sixty seconds, an adolescent attempts suicide—one in two hundred succeed. These are scary numbers. They mean that suicide kills far more teens and young adults than do such dread diseases as cancer and heart ailments. Only accidents and homicides claim more young lives. To adults, these numbers are especially astounding because we'd like to think that our kids' teen years are carefree, fun, and exciting. But the truth is that along with the fun come pressures and fears so strong that for some teens they far outweigh the joys of life.

In almost all cases, suicide is the solution of last resort. It is the cry for help when all other cries have been ignored. A suicide attempt is a way of shouting, "Hey, look at me. Help me. I can't go on. Listen to me so that I may live." Suicide becomes a way of communicating with others after all other forms of communication have broken down. (The process of communicating through suicide is different for boys than it is for girls. Of all teen suicide attempts, 90 percent are made by girls, but of all successful suicides, 70 percent are boys.)

If you have decided that your teen is depressed, you should talk about suicide. Bringing it out in the open immediately lets your teen know that you're listening to the disguised cries for help.

THE MYTHS OF SUICIDE

Before you begin, take a little time to clarify your own feelings and dispel some of the common myths surrounding suicides:

Myth: You shouldn't talk about suicide to a depressed person; it will give her ideas.

Reality: If suicide is on your teen's mind, it's vital to get that fact out in the open. This immediately takes away the mystery and the secrecy that can make suicide appealing to a teenager. If your teen is not thinking about suicide, mentioning that some teens do consider this a solution to depression will simply show your teen that you understand that teenagers have very real, strong feelings. It will show you are not appalled or disgusted by the idea but rather are open to talking about it. Suicide is the topic of many popular songs, music videos, and movies for teens. Bringing up the subject when your teen is depressed will not plant a new idea.

Myth: People who talk about suicide never do it.
Reality: Talking about suicide is a warning; take it seriously. If your teen yells, "I wish I were dead!" don't ignore it. Call her back when she's calmer and talk about the feelings that caused her to say that. (See the next section for tips on what to say.)

Myth: An unsuccessful suicide attempt will embarrass the person into not trying again.
Reality: Suicide statistics prove this is false. The first attempt is the hardest. Once an attempt has been made, a person who does not get help is very likely to try again.

Myth: Happiness after a depression removes the risk of suicide.
Reality: It is often the case that people attempt or commit suicide after a period of calm and happiness. Friends remark, "I'm so surprised, because she finally got over her depression." Often the happiness follows the decision to opt for death. This ends the internal struggle and brings a sense of peace. Don't be fooled by a sudden lift in mood.

Myth: People who attempt suicide want to die.
Reality: Many people who make suicide attempts have no intention of dying. They are shouting for help using a suicide method that gives them the greatest chance for rescue. They may take a small dosage of pills that could be barely lethal. They turn on the gas in a closed room, but leave open a crack in the window. They make superficial slashes on their wrist. (Those more determined to die

usually use more violent and destructive methods, such as guns or hanging.) But this is a thin line: many die who didn't really plan to, and many are saved after the most violent attempt.

HOW TO TALK ABOUT SUICIDE

It can be very difficult to fund just the right words to talk about suicide. The following suggestions will help you broach the subjuct with sensitivity and love.

Ask Questions

Be frank and ask your teen directly if she is thinking of suicide. It is often a relief for an adolescent to admit having such ideas. When you bring up the subject, it gives your teen the opening she needs to talk about her "secret" feelings. The answer to this question will also help you evaluate the seriousness of the situation.

When you bring up the subject, start slowly. Ask:

"You seem down lately. Are you feeling depressed?"
"Does life sometimes seem like it's not worth living?"
"Have you ever thought about ending it all by killing yourself?"
"Have you thought about how you would do it?"
"Would you like to talk to someone who's trained to help teens
  deal with these kinds of feelings?"

Listen

Listening is the single most helpful thing you can do. Listen with full attention. Sit facing your teen. Look in her eyes. Listen with compassion, not judgment. Don't interrupt; just listen. You must let your child get her problem out in the open before you can begin analyzing it. Let her be angry, hurt, and hopeless before you offer ways to cope. Having time to vent these feelings is a step toward dealing with them.

If your teen tells you she is not thinking about suicide, don't push the issue. (It's very possible the thought never entered her mind!) Still, use this opportunity to share what you know about other teens who chose suicide to deal with their depression. Use the statistics given in this chapter to explain why you asked in the first place. Then continue the conversation with the suggestions that follow. All teens need to know that their parents care and that there are many constructive ways to solve problems.

Show You Care

To counter her feelings of worthlessness, tell your teen that you love her and that she is not alone in this. Tell her that she is loved for being herself, not for what she accomplishes. Stay nearby during this difficult time and keep letting her know you care.

Balance Emotions with Reason

Your teen needs you to stay strong and reasonable. While being understanding and compassionate, you can also be the voice of reason that touches her unbalanced emotional frame of mind. Things you might say include the following:

"Problems are temporary, and things change."
"You feel awful now, but you can't know how you'll feel one year or five years from now."
"So many others have felt the way you do; then the feeling passes or they get help through counseling, and they go on to live happy lives."

"It's not crazy or strange to feel so depressed. Many people feel this way at one time or another."

BE CAREFUL WHAT YOU SAY

Suicide is a sensitive issue, so think before you respond when your teen yells, "You'll be sorry when I'm dead." Try to avoid these common mistakes when talking to your teen about suicide:

Don't act shocked or scared: "Oh my God! Don't say that!"

Don't try to reassure: "There's nothing to worry about."

Don't try to shame your teen out of the idea: "Suicide is cowardly. You have been given such a good life, you ought to be ashamed to even think about such an idea."

Don't call his bluff: "Don't say something so stupid. You're not gonna kill yourself." Or: "Go ahead. Kill yourself if you think that will help."

Don't treat the idea lightly: "Oh, come on; your problems aren't that bad."

Don't try to analyze the reason: "You're just saying that to get my attention." Or: "You're always so dramatic."

Don't try to ignore or minimize the problem: "Why don't you get a good night's sleep; you'll feel better in the morning."

GETTING PROFESSIONAL HELP

Even if you are successful in getting your teen to talk to you about suicidal feelings, it is important to get professional help. Even if your teen, who has expressed suicidal thoughts, thanks you for your interest and promises that she feels much better now, get professional help. Many adolescents will purposely mislead those trying to help them by acting as though the crisis has passed. Whenever a serious risk of suicide exists, get help from a suicide prevention center (available in most communities), a suicide hotline (which can be found in the phone book under "Suicide"), your school guidance office, or a mental health professional. If your teen refuses help, go for help yourself and ask for advice on how to handle the situation. And always keep talking to your teen. It is when teens are most difficult and obstinate that they need us the most.

RESOURCES

Covenant House NINELINE
(800) 999-9999
Crisis intervention, referral, and information services for troubled teens and families

Mental Health Net
Web site: http://www.cmhc.com
General guide to on-line mental health topics

Youth Crisis Hotline
(800) 448-4663
Counseling and referrals for teens in crisis

FOR FURTHER READING

Herskowitz, Joel. *Is Your Child Depressed?* New York: Warner Books, 1988.
Williams, Kate. *A Parent's Guide for Suicidal and Depressed Teens.* Center City, Minn.: Hazelden, 1995.

Especially for Teens

Maloney, Michael, and others. *Straight Talk About Anxiety and Depression*. New York: Facts on File, 1991.

Silverstein, Alvin, Virginia Nunn, and Laura Nunn. *Depression*. Springfield, N.J.: Enslow, 1997.

Ethics,
Moral Values, and Religion

Jake's friends were very excited. They had the answers to Friday's final exam. "Come on over, Jake," Mike yelled into the phone. "We're all making a copy and then celebrating. There's no reason to stay stuck in the house studying this week!" Jake hesitated. He knew it was wrong to cheat on an exam, but everybody else was going to get a good grade without studying—why shouldn't he?

Our teens often face moral dilemmas that are very hard to solve. They're finding out that being a "good kid" no longer means keeping the room clean or doing homework on time; now it means facing tough ethical situations and doing what's right even when it's not popular or easy. This is probably the most difficult task our children face as teenagers. They can't do it unless they know for sure that moral and religious values are not old-fashioned. They need to know that these values are the foundation of our civilization. They make our society function. They are the core of a good and happy life.

But how will they know this? Current TV, music, magazines, novels, and newspapers bombard them with immoral messages. Their friends are in the same boat; their neighbors are shut up behind closed doors; their extended family usually lives far away. There's only one person left who can pass on the importance of positive character traits and moral values—you. If teenagers are going to internalize these things, they must know what they are. They must have them spelled out in words and deeds.

There are many character traits, ethics, and moral values that you certainly want to nurture in your children. We have chosen to discuss kindness, integrity, honesty, perseverance, and optimism. We offer these as examples and encourage you to use these ideas as springboards from which to discuss other values that are important to your family.

We should add a word of caution here. Even if you are exemplary models of high moral beliefs and even if you work hard to pass these beliefs on to your teens, they may not be receptive to all your ideas. Don't get discouraged. Because they are trying so hard to separate from you, they may think they have to rebel against what you think is good. But your lessons are not wasted. Through your example and open discussions, you are providing your teens with the basis of beliefs they will return to when they are finished rebelling. Give them this home base whether they seem to want it or not. It will always be there as a point of reference in the future.

HOW AND WHEN TO TALK ABOUT CHARACTER TRAITS AND MORAL VALUES

Just by watching and listening, your teens have been learning for years about the character traits and moral values that are important to you. They have already picked up your own ethical standards, and they know what things you value. But now, as they begin to develop an independent spirit, it's a good time to talk about these things, to bring out in the open what you assume they know but have never discussed.

You speak loudest through example. There's no way around the fact that you cannot talk about character traits and moral values and act in ways that contradict your message. Now that your teens have a more adultlike way of thinking about the world and what makes it work, the "Do as I say, not as I do" method of teaching will destroy any hope of leading your kids to high moral ground. If you haven't been a good model of ethics and values up to this point, now is the time to begin. It's not too late—there's still time. If you have led a quiet, moral life up to this point, now is the time to talk about what you do and explain why you do it. No one else is showing your kids what's right and wrong or what's good and bad. It's up to you.

The ups and downs of daily life give you a wealth of opportunities to bring up a discussion of character traits and moral values. When you hear your kids talking cruelly about another teen, when you see your teen struggling with a decision, when your child has been hurt by the cruelty of others, use these experiences as teaching opportunities. Each of the sections that follow offers an example of day-to-day dilemmas that can be used for further discussion. Most do not have "right" or "wrong" answers; they simply offer topics for discussion. In addition, keep your eyes and ears open for the things that are going on in your teen's life that will open the door to more heart-to-hearts.

WHAT TO SAY ABOUT KINDNESS

Kindness is the ability to show concern, sympathy, and understanding. It means putting the needs and desires of others first. Can you imagine if future generations had no concept of kindness? What a hard life it would be for everyone. Your teen needs to see the value of kindness every day.

Your kids learn how to treat people with kindness in two ways: (1) they watch how you treat others, and (2) they watch how you treat them.

Talk About How You Treat Others

How many opportunities do you have each day to treat others, outside your family, kindly? In the hectic rush of family life, you may think there are few opportunities, but in fact there are hundreds. Taking advantage of just a few of these opportunities will speak loudly about your views on kindness.

You Speak Volumes About Kindness When You Volunteer to Help Others. Kindness means you care about something beyond yourself. It encourages you to reach out and help others. It requires that you are not self-centered. The best way to teach these lessons is to work together with others toward a common good. If you are a volunteer, talk about the work you do. Explain why you do it. Bring your teen with you when possible. Also encourage your teen to get into the volunteer spirit herself. Teens' schedules can be very busy, but there's always some group or organization that can use two willing hands on any schedule. Volunteers are busy in hundreds of civic and social fields; your teens might enjoy health care, politics, environmental protection, education, drug awareness, or helping the hungry and homeless. (Volunteering also has the personal benefit of giving teens experience in areas they might like to pursue as a career.) Call your local United Way Volunteer Center; they can put you on the right track.

You Talk to Your Teens About Kindness Every Time You Talk to Other People. We show kindness not only in the major efforts of volunteering to help those less fortunate but also in every human transaction. When the sales clerk says, "Have a nice day," look her in the eye before rushing away and say, "You too." When someone tries to cut you off in traffic, don't swear; instead say, "This person seems to be in more of a hurry than I am; I'd better let him in." When a telemarketer calls on the phone with an offer you're not interested in, don't slam down the phone; instead give a polite refusal: "Thank you for calling, but I'm not interested. Have a good day. Good-bye." Every time you speak to another person within earshot of your teens, you also speak to your teens.

You Talk to Your Teens About Kindness Every Time You Talk About Other People. In family conversations, try your best to speak kindly about others, or say nothing at all. Teenagers learn to criticize, condemn, or gossip about others from your example. Don't give people such labels as *stupid, evil, lazy,* or *no good.* If instead you praise others and find the good in them, your teens will learn how to affirm and celebrate the dignity and worth of all human beings.

Talk About How You Treat Your Teens

Although you will never say, "Right now I'm treating you kindly. This is how you should treat others," your actions deliver this message very clearly. In order for teens to show kindness to others, they must feel safe, valuable, and respected themselves. You fill your children with these feelings every time you show kindness to them. Every time you listen to their ideas and acknowledge their feelings. Every time you say, "I know this is important to you, so let's talk about it."

Talk About Day-to-Day Dilemmas Involving Kindness
   • Tell your teens that you read about a teenager who committed suicide because her classmates had been teasing her every day about being overweight. Ask your teens:

> "Why do you think teenagers would intentionally be so cruel to a classmate?"
> "Does this happen in your school?"
> "What would you do if your friends started teasing a classmate because of his or her appearance?"

   • Tell your teens that your own friends started gossiping about another friend who was not with the group. Ask them, "What do you think I should do in that situation?" "What would you do?"
   • Tell your teens that there is a blood drive going on at the local blood bank. Ask them, "Do you think I should give blood?" If they are old enough to donate, ask, "Do you want to give blood?"

WHAT TO SAY ABOUT INTEGRITY

Having integrity means that a person is the same on the inside as he or she claims to be on the outside. It is something that gives peace of mind and gains the admiration of all others. We have many opportunities each day to teach the basics of integrity—right from wrong and honest from dishonest—through example and precept.

   Having integrity means being reliable and true to your word. Your teens live in a world where "I'll call you later" means "never." Where "I'll meet you at eight" means "Maybe I'll be there when I get there." Where "I promise" means nothing. You can show them through example and by your expectations that this is not the way a person with integrity acts. If you say, "I'll pick you up at two," do it. If you say, "I'll come to your game on Saturday," be there. Our kids get a skewed picture of honesty and reliability when they often hear, "I know I promised to drive you to the mall tonight, but I'm really tired. You understand, don't you? I promise I'll take you next week." And, "I know I said I'd be at your performance, but the boss called a late meeting and then I got caught up in traffic. You know how it is." And on and on.

The most difficult part about teaching kids about integrity is the black-and-white aspect of it described in the old saying, "There are no degrees of honesty. Either you are honest or you are not." This is hard to accept when everyone around you is getting ahead by rationalizing dishonest actions that give them the advantage: cheating on tests, taking steroids to improve athletic performance, lying to get their way, and so on. You can help your kids stand tall in these circumstances by repeatedly telling them: "Wrong is wrong, even when everyone is doing it. Right is right, even when no one is doing it."

Talk About Day-to-Day Dilemmas Involving Integrity

• Tell your teens you heard on the news about two kids who found $500 in the park. The kids gave the money to the police, but the other kids from their neighborhood who were interviewed said the kids who found the money were crazy for not keeping it. Ask your teens, "What do you think?" "What would you do?" (This is a real news story.)

• Tell your teens you went shopping today, and the clerk gave you the wrong change. Ask them what they think you should have done. What if it was too much change? What if it was too little change?

• Tell your teens you know of someone who was asked by her boss to lie to a customer. Ask your teens, "Should she do it to keep her job?" "Is there ever a situation where lying would be the right solution?"

• Ask your teens, "What would you do if your friend called and told you he had the answer sheet to tomorrow's test?"

WHAT TO SAY ABOUT RESPONSIBILITY

A sense of responsibility makes us accountable for our actions and therefore trustworthy. This trait is becoming harder to develop in our young because they are growing up in a world where it seems that no one is responsible for anything. No one is personally guilty of anything, according to the news: I am not responsible because I am poor. Because I gained wealth too quickly and too early. Because I was abused, underprivileged, or overprivileged. Because I ate too much sugar. Because my parents were too permissive. Because my parents were too demanding.

The excuses are endless. Your teens need your help to realize that it is the courageous, morally correct thing to take responsibility for one's actions.

Make sure the rules in your house are clear. Tell your teens:

"If you drop something, pick it up. If you break something, replace it. If you make a mess, clean it up."
"There are consequences for actions. Face up to the consequences of what you do without blaming others."
"Don't deny your actions. If you did it, be brave enough to say so."

Talk About Day-to-Day Dilemmas Involving Responsibility

• Tell your teens about the court case in Florida in which the young defendant pleaded innocent and blamed the excess sugar in

Twinkies for his violent outburst. Ask your teen if this is a reasonable defense.

• Point out litter on the roadside or in your parks and ask your teen who should be responsible for cleaning it up.

• If your teen does poorly on a school assignment, be sure to ask who's to blame for this. The response will tell you a lot about your teen's view of personal responsibility.

• Ask your teen if he or she knows why teens are asked to do family chores.

WHAT TO SAY ABOUT PERSEVERANCE

Perseverance makes things happen. It makes us try again when we fail. It lets us stand up when we're knocked down. It keep us out of the group called "quitters." It is not something that always comes naturally. The quick response to a challenge may be to give up, but with your help, your teens can learn to keep trying in the face of adversity. "Hang in there" is more than an expression of encouragement to someone experiencing hardship or difficulty; it is sound advice for anyone intent on doing good in the world.

Talk About Day-to-Day Dilemmas Involving Perseverance

• Ask your teen if she thinks it's right for a ball player to quit a team in the middle of the season because the team hasn't won a single game.

• Ask your teen if he knows anyone who is really very smart but who gets poor grades in school. If he does, ask your teen why he thinks someone would not try to do his or her best.

• Ask your teen why, considering that it's obviously easier to give up when things get tough, some people persevere and try again and again.

WHAT TO SAY ABOUT OPTIMISM

Optimism produces resilience even in the face of setbacks; it allows a child to meet and exceed goals and expectations. Pessimism, in contrast, can numb a child to the pleasures of life and keep her from achieving her goals; it can even take a toll on her physical health.

Martin Seligman, a psychologist at the University of Pennsylvania and coauthor of *The Optimistic Child*, has spent more than twenty-five years researching why some people are motivated and optimistic, whereas others are easily discouraged. According to Seligman, how people respond to setbacks—optimistically or pessimistically—is a fairly accurate indicator of how well they will succeed in school, in sports, and in certain kinds of work. He has also learned that children who are optimists tend to think that any setback, such as a grade on a test that was lower than hoped for, is temporary—the result of a particular circumstance, such as not studying enough. Pessimistic children tend to experience any setback as permanent; a low grade, they believe, reflects their overall lack of intelligence and ability.

You can nurture your own optimistic spirit if you spend some time each day working on these three steps to more positive thinking:

1. Recognize the thoughts that flit through your mind when you feel bad. Let's say, for example, that when you find out you have to stay late at work to finish a report, you immediately think, "I hate this job. I never get home on time."
2. Evaluate these automatic thoughts. You'll find that they are not necessarily accurate. Stop a thought like "I hate this job" dead in its tracks and ask yourself if it's really true.

3. Generate more accurate explanations when bad things happen. Use these accurate explanations to challenge your automatic thoughts. Adjust your feelings to admit that you hate when you have to work late but that the job itself isn't so bad, and that you work late only a few days each month.

In three quick mental steps you've changed an irrational pessimistic reaction to an optimistic one based in reality. (Optimists aren't always happy about everything that happens to them, but they do have the mental ability to keep everyday annoyances from turning into mental catastrophes!)

Once you've got the knack of stopping negative thoughts and challenging them, give your teen a chance to try it too. When your teen faces a problem or challenge, get him to recognize his optimistic or pessimistic style of responding.

Suppose your teen, who has a lot of homework to do, complains, "I hate school. I never get a chance to hang out with my friends!" Help him think about the real problem and how to solve it:

1. Identify the real problem: Does he really hate school? Or is he angry that he can't be with his friends right now?
2. Challenge the belief that he *never* gets to hang out with his friends.
3. Think about the real consequence of working longer on homework. Help him see that he'll feel happy when he goes to school prepared. He'll be able to hang out with his friends a little later or the next day.

Help your kids go through this three-step exercise whenever you hear pessimistic remarks. It takes a while to realize that the first thing that flashes through the mind may not be a true picture of the situation.

Talk About Day-to-Day Dilemmas Involving Optimism

• Ask your teen why she thinks people who have never won a single lottery still buy tickets.

• Ask your teen if she thinks people should plan outdoor weddings when one can never be sure of the weather.

• Ask your teen whether, if five bad things happened to him in a row, he would expect something good or bad to happen next.

TALK ABOUT RELIGION

Undoubtedly we will meet with resistance as we try to instill admirable character traits, ethics, and moral values in our teens. They'll want to know, "Why should I act differently than my friends?" "Why should I do what's right when everyone else is getting away with being dishonest?" The answers to these kinds of questions can come from many sources. They may come from your own firm belief in the power of moral and ethical living for its own sake, or they may come from your religious beliefs. In some families, a belief in a higher power and a life of spirituality offers sound guidelines for making ethical and moral decisions. In other families, a tradition of organized religion provides the answers. If you have raised your children within an established religious community, the following section will help you find the answers when your teens begin to question their faith.

Research tells us that teens who receive the gift of faith from their parents have an advantage over those who don't. One such study was conducted by Peter L. Benson, Ph.D., president of the Search Institute in Minneapolis. Benson conducted a survey of forty-seven thousand students in grades six through twelve and found that as a child's involvement in religion increases, all types of high-risk behavior decrease. He also found that there's less drug use, antisocial behavior, and early sexual involvement and more empathy and volunteerism in children who follow their faith. Many experts agree that the values conveyed by most religions, such as love, mercy, and kindness, are easier to convey within a religious context.

And there's more good news for teens of faith. A study in the *Journal of Youth and Adolescence* reported that teens who attended church frequently and who viewed their religions as providing meaning for their lives had lower incidence of depression than their peers. These researchers found religion to be a positive force in the lives of adolescents.

For many parents, religiously based moral convictions and codes of right and wrong are legacies they pass on to their children. But how do teens relate to the family religion? This is a question we must try to answer to help our teens continue in their spiritual growth through these rebellious and questioning years. The details of your conversations will vary depending on your religious beliefs, of course. But if you are a religious family and wonder how you can keep your teen tuned into the faith, the following topics will give you a good place to start.

Talk About Your Own Beliefs

The best place to start a conversation about religion is with the focus on yourself and your own beliefs. You can't assume your children know these things—you have to talk out loud about your faith.

- Be sure to talk to your kids about the sustenance you have found in daily religious experiences. When you are sad or anxious, say, "I don't know what I'd do at a time like this if I didn't have God to talk to."

- Talk about God as someone who is ever present in your day—not someone far away and unapproachable. Say, "I find myself talking to God so often during the day. I find Him to be a very good listener."

- Tell them about your religious convictions and the values you live by. "When my prayers aren't answered, I still have faith that God has heard me. I have to assume His answer is no."

- When you have a major decision to make, let your kids know that you believe in the power of prayer. Say, "I'm praying for guidance on this. I'm sure God will help me decide what to do."

If you do not live your religion, your teen will know that it is not an important family value. In this case, you have little chance of convincing your child to practice the faith with any personal belief or conviction.

Talk About the Value of Faith

As in all things, teens want to know what's in it for them. When you talk about religion, be sure to bring up the value of faith:

Religious faith satisfies the need to have something to believe in, something that gives meaning to life and death.

Religion offers a sense of justice, a sense that in the end, good is rewarded and evil is punished.

Religion gives consolation and comfort in adversity.

Faith in God reminds us that we are loved and are of ines-
timable worth. (This can bolster a teen's self-esteem and
promote reverence for life.)

Religion advocates the brotherhood of humanity.

Talk About Doubts

Teenagers doubt everything they hear from adults. It's their way of
pulling away from total dependence and reaching out mentally to
create their own life. Religion is usually not spared the critical ax of
adolescence. This is normal, so don't despair if your teen says, "I
don't believe in God." Give her the opportunity to talk about her
doubts and ask questions in an environment that encourages the
spiritual journey. A teen's doubting is not blasphemy—it is growth.
Give her the freedom to ask any question at all. If you are patient
and understanding and continue to show a solid example of your
own faith, your teen will come out on the other side of the doubt
with a faith that is stronger and more personally satisfying.

If your teen says: "Just because you believe in God doesn't mean I
have to."
You say: "That's true. You do have to decide for yourself if you
believe in God. If you do not, can you tell me why? What are your
reasons?"

If your teen says: "I don't get anything out of religious services."
You say: "It's not about you getting something out of it; it's about
you putting something into it. That's what a religious service is all
about." (This should be followed by a review of what an individual
can bring to your religious service.)

If your teen says: "Why is there evil in the world?"
You say: "God has given us free will to choose good or evil, and even though we are strengthened when we choose good, some people don't."

If your teen says: "How can a loving God allow poverty, disease, and war?"
You say: "I don't understand it either, but I have faith that God knows what He is doing."

If your teen says: "Why should I go to a church where the people are hypocrites? I see church members being deceitful during the week and then praying on the weekend."
You say: "Even religious people are human. They struggle and sometimes do the wrong thing. Only with God's help can they find the honest path, so it's a good thing that they return to pray."

If your teen asks a question that you simply can't answer, say so. Say:

"That's a question people have been asking since time began. What do you think the answer might be? Let's see if we can research this and find the answer."

Religion is a gift we give our children. We have no way of knowing what they will do with it, but we know that if they accept this gift, they can gain an understanding of their place in the world, a sense of spiritual wholeness, and a home base of comfort and security to come back to whenever they need it.

FOR FURTHER READING

Coles, Robert. *The Moral Intelligence of Children*. New York: Random House, 1998.

Dosick, Wayne. *Golden Rules*. San Francisco: HarperSanFrancisco, 1995.

Higgins, Kevin, and Phil Landrum. *Guiding Your Teen to a Faith That Lasts*. Grand Rapids, Mich.: Discovery House, 1994.

Lee, Steve, and Chap Clark. *Boys to Men: How Fathers Can Help Build Character in Their Sons*. Chicago: Moody Press, 1995.

Especially for Teens
Canfield, Jack, and others. *Chicken Soup for the Teenage Soul*. Deerfield Beach, Fla.: Health Communications, 1997.

DiGeronimo, Theresa Foy. *A Student's Guide to Volunteering*. Franklin Lakes, N.J.: Career Press, 1995.

Shellenberger, Susie. *Camp, Car Washes, Heaven, and Hell (Pretty Important Ideas on Living God's Way)*. Minneapolis, Minn.: Bethany House, 1996.

Gangs

The signs around town were unavoidable—teen gangs were staking out their turfs. There were graffiti on public walls, fights at the high school sports events, and kids in gang jackets on the street corners. Now Sue Jonas noticed her own son was doodling gang symbols on his textbook covers. When she warned him that gangs were dangerous, he laughed at her. What else could she say?

WHAT IS A GANG?

The history of gangs is an old one. Socrates complained about gangs in Greece four hundred years before the birth of Christ. Ever since, history is full of stories about bands of young people who prey on people weaker than themselves. This is no comfort to any parent whose teen joins a gang or to the law enforcement agencies who are trying to keep track of the damage gangs cause. The U.S. Department of Justice estimates that as many as 125,000 to 250,000 young people are members of gangs. This figure does not include as many as 750,000 "wannabes," or aspiring gang members.

Gang membership is not confined to certain types of people. Anyone—male or female, wealthy or low income, from a functional or dysfunctional family—can join a gang. Renowned and organized gangs are setting up chapters in thousands of small cities, while copycat gangs are blossoming in small towns and suburbs. Police are noticing that the age of gang members is dropping. This used to be a problem related to high school students; now middle school and elementary school kids are often recruited. The national popularity of gangsta rap music, which glorifies violence, abuse of women, and disrespect for authority, has helped spread the culture of gangs, cutting across class, economic, racial, and geographic lines.

Let's try to define what we mean by *gang*. In a 1991 survey of more than seventy gang prevention programs, the National Crime Prevention Council used the following five groupings to categorize gangs:

1. *Traditional street gangs*, such as the Bloods, the Crips, the El Rukns, or the Black Gangster Disciples
2. *Neighborhood gangs* (sometimes called posses) that are generally more informal and have no areawide or regional reach
3. *Ethnic gangs* that base membership on cultural traditions or ethnic identity or heritage
4. *Drug dealer gangs* formed or currently organized to generate income through the drug trade
5. *Hate gangs*, generally motivated by some form of ethnic, racial, or social bias (Skinheads are considered to be part of the fastest-growing hate group in the nation, which is made up almost entirely of people ages sixteen to twenty-five.)

Gangs may also include smaller, less notorious groups in any neighborhood or high school. These include the high school fraternities and sororities and any other loosely organized group that roams city or suburban streets. Even teens who join satanic cults are often categorized as gangs rather than as cults because most teens dabble in satanism as a means of social rebellion rather than as a religious commitment. (See "Cults" for more information.) The National Crime Prevention Council defines *gang* as a group of people who form an allegiance, to the exclusion of others, for common purposes and who engage in violent, unlawful, antisocial, or criminal activity. Police on the streets now say that gangs are shedding the label of *gang* and taking on the name *street organization* or *street association*. Whatever the name, this subject gives us something important to talk to our teens about. It presents a dangerous and unlawful situation that our kids need to know about before they find themselves in too deep to get out.

WHY TEENS JOIN GANGS

Before you can tell your teenagers why they should not belong to a gang, take some time to consider why they would even want to claim membership in this kind of peer group. There are, in fact, many legitimate reasons that have to do with the psychological needs of any teenager. What gang recruiters promise is not exceptional or exotic. The promises speak to very basic human needs. Kids ache to belong, to be supported, and to be cared about; some kids are willing to risk death for that. The gang recruiters can teach us something if we listen to what they offer in the areas that are so important to all teens: identity, acceptance, authority, sexuality, power, and safety.

Identity and Acceptance

The teen years are a time for a young person to discover the answers to two important questions: Who am I? and Who am I separate from my parents and my family? This is a time of self-consciousness and a preoccupation with self. It is a time when the need to belong and feel secure in self is very strong. In fact, self-esteem and acceptance by peers are closely related. Attachments to peers help the teen let go of old ways relating to their families. That's why most young people prefer to spend more time with friends than with family.

Gangs give a concrete identity that members can hold on to. "I am a member of this group. I dress like them. I look like them, and I act like them. I look at them and know who I am." Gangs also offer the opportunity to belong to an intimate peer group. Their activities gain them attention from teachers, parents, and peers. A teen who was an invisible, ordinary student puts on a gang symbol and becomes part of an insider's group, someone recognized and even feared. The feeling of belonging is increased by the gang's exclusion of those who don't belong. This is why gangs thrive on secrecy, secret codes, handshakes, and symbols.

Authority

Part of separating from the family includes testing and rebelling against authority. In some teens this takes relatively mild forms such as testing curfew or saying things to push parental buttons. For other teens, the struggle against authority involves higher-risk behaviors that include criminal activities, sexual promiscuity, unsafe driving, and drug use.

Gangs offer support for acting out against authority. They give teens encouragement to defy social and moral norms for the sake of defiance. Whether through loitering or drug trafficking, gangs thrive on teenagers' need to challenge authority.

Sexuality

All teens have a heightened awareness of their sexuality. They need to experiment with boundaries, behaviors, and forms of intimacy. Because gangs encourage members to defy conventional norms, self-gratification through sexual activity or even abuse become accepted (and sometimes required).

Power

Power has magnetic appeal to many teens. They live in an in-between world where they are no longer children but not yet adults. They are physically mature but emotionally immature. They struggle developmentally for some separation from parents. Yet they are powerless to achieve this independence; after all, they still live at home with parents, have to attend school every day, have limited incomes, and have a curfew. In the face of powerlessness, all teens seek out places where they do have some power, some ability to influence their environment.

Gang members gain a feeling of power in many ways. They gain power over adults and peers who are afraid of them. They gain power over authorities by breaking laws and getting away with it. They gain power through the freedom to indulge in deviant, criminal, or sexual activity.

Safety

If violent gangs are in your neighborhood and school, your teens may feel they need to join a gang to protect themselves from harm. Gangs promise safety and security.

Although all teens struggle with these issues of identity, acceptance, authority, sexuality, power, and safety, not all join gangs to help them cope. Some find strength and encouragement in their families. Some turn to close friends. Some turn to organized activities such as band, church youth groups, and sports. But teens with the fewest resources and those with weak coping skills are often prey for gangs. When kids are asked why they belong to a gang, they often give the same reasons. These teens say:

> They care about me.
> They pay attention to me.
> They make me feel important.
> They make me feel like I belong.
> They give me protection.

Gang members really want nothing more than any other teen does. But they find these things in dangerous places.

WHY WE MUST TALK TO TEENS ABOUT GANGS

Gangs aren't something that "can't affect my kids." Based on a survey released by the National Center for Education Statistics in 1998, nearly twice as many teenagers reported gangs in their schools in 1995 as they did in 1989. The author noted that the gang increase occurred in every type of community. Wherever kids band together with nothing else to do but cause trouble, the possibility of gang activity exists. We should all talk to our kids about this problem.

If gangs are in your neighborhood or schools, you must help your teens see their downside. From a distance, gangs offer so many things teens psychologically need that your child needs your help to see past the illusion. The following ideas for conversations should give you a starting point from which to get your teen talking and thinking. Don't try to cover everything in one sitting. Try one topic and see where the discussion takes you before you jump into the next.

Talk About Your Values. Remind your children that they live in a free country where people should always have the right to walk down the street without fear—and gangs take away that right. Remind them that all people are equal and that no one should have to be intimidated by others—and gangs place themselves above the law and thrive on intimidation.

Talk About Violence. Tell your teens: "Gangs do not offer a shelter from violence. They cause violence." The bigger a gang gets, the more violent it is likely to be and the more likely to carry weapons. Smaller gangs begin with knives, chains, razors, and clubs. Larger gangs get into handguns, pistols, and automatic rifles. The violent gangs don't just carry weapons for show—they use them. They use them against each other and against innocent people who cross them or happen to be in their way. The bottom line is, gangs can be deadly. The Los Angeles County Sheriff's Department estimated that gangs kill at least one person in their city every single day. This isn't a safe way to live.

Talk About Drug Dealing. The most notorious gangs are nothing more than organized drug rings. And even the smallest gangs in small towns usually find themselves mixed up in drug use and dealing. Tell your kids:

"Drugs are deadly and illegal. If you ever join a gang that uses or sells drugs, you will eventually find yourself in jail—or dead. The quick

money you make or the highs you get are not worth giving up what
you could make of your life in the future. You get involved with
gangs and drugs, you're at a dead end. There's no place else to go."

(See "Drugs" for more information.)

Talk About Exclusion and Hatred. Only the "right" kind of
person can belong to a gang. This exclusion and hate of others is
called prejudice. Tell your teens: "Prejudice is what killed thousands
of Jewish people during the Holocaust. Prejudice is what killed
Martin Luther King. Prejudice is what tears a country, a town, and
a school apart." Be firm and clear. Let your teens know: "I do not
want you in a biased or hateful group." (See "Prejudice" for more
information.)

Explore the Effects of Gangs on People and Communities.
Point out that gangs affect the quality of life for everybody. Resi-
dents are intimated by gang members. This means that people seek
refuge inside their homes and no longer feel safe on the streets. They
no longer go for walks in the park. They no longer enjoy the basic
freedom to go where they please in safety. Even businesses are affected. As gangs hang out on the street and frighten people away,
businesses lose customers. Larger gangs often demand "protection"
money from small business owners. Many businesses are repeatedly
robbed by gang members. All these things force businesses to close
down or move out of town, which takes jobs and economic opportunity away from the community. We all pay a heavy price.

Talk About Personal Freedom and Individuality. *Tell your
teen:* "Now that you're a teenager, you've earned the right to have
some independence and think for yourself. Gangs take away that

right. You're no longer an individual who can say no or 'I don't want to.' Gang members are property, not free people."

After your discussion, make it simple: give your teens three good reasons to stay out of gangs. Tell them:

1. "I disapprove of gangs."
2. "I don't want to see you hurt or arrested."
3. "I think you are special and worth protecting."

TALKING TO TEENS ALREADY INVOLVED IN A GANG

The National Crime Prevention Council advises that if you notice the following signs of gang involvement, you should suspect that your child has joined a gang:

Changes in type of friends
Changes in dress habits, such as wearing the same color combination all the time
Gang symbols on books or clothing
Tattoos
Secretiveness about activities
Extra cash from unknown sources
Carrying a weapon
Declining interest in school and family
Being arrested or detained by the police

What to Do
If your teen has joined a gang, don't back off but don't attack either. You have no hope of reasoning with your teen if you yell or demand.

Take a calmer approach and do a lot of listening. Tell your teen: "I'm interested in your group. Tell me more about them." The goal is to start some kind of dialogue.

If your teen says: "They're not a gang."
You say: "Can only certain people join? Do they meet in secret? Do they protect their turf?" If the answers are yes, they are a gang.

If your teen says: "I want to belong to this organization."
You say: "Tell me why. What are the benefits? What are the dangers?"

If your teen says: "I have to join a gang for protection."
You say: "That may not necessarily be true. Most gang violence is committed against other gang members. In the gang, you're forced to fight others, and you're identified as a target for other gangs to attack. You don't need the protection of the gang until you join it. If you want to stay out of dangerous situations, you should stay out of the gang. Do you really want to belong to this gang?"

If your teen says: "As a member of this gang, I've got it made!"
You say: "I'm not sure I understand how this is true. You know the gang will ask you to do things that are dangerous or illegal. You might even be killed. How is that 'having it made'?"

If your teen says: "They are my friends."
You say: "Gang members aren't true friends. Friends don't force each other to do things that are against the law. Friends give each other choices. Friends want what is best in life for each other. Friends stay friends only for as long as they want to. They are free to find other friends. In a gang, members are at the mercy of the leaders. I don't think this is friendship."

If your teen says: "You don't understand me or my friends."
You say: "You're probably right, but I'd really like to know more. Tell me."

If your teen says: "It's none of your business."
You say: "That isn't true. Any decisions you make about a gang can endanger every member of this family. Any violent act aimed at you can come right to our door and affect your brothers and sisters, as well as me. It's also my business because I am your parent and I am legally and morally responsible for your welfare. It's also my business because I love you."

Whenever possible, don't fight over gang membership. This makes your teen more determined to defy you. Instead, listen more. Give responses like these: "Tell me more about that." "Why do you think that?" "What do you think will happen?" The answers to these kinds of questions will help your teen sort out his own feelings. They'll make him think and analyze the risks and rewards of gang membership. With your help, he may decide for himself that the benefits just don't make up for the danger.

AN ACTION PLAN

It is very important that all parents talk to their kids about the issue of gangs. But if gangs are in your neighborhood or schools, it is also very important that you act in ways that will keep your kids out of gangs. Many gang members say they joined because the gang offered them support, caring, and a sense of order and purpose—all things most parents try to give their kids. The odds are that the better you meet these needs, the less need your teenagers will see for gangs. Here are some parenting skills offered by the National Crime Prevention Council that are especially important:

- Talk with and listen to your child. Spend some special time with each child.
- Put a high value on education and help your child to do his or her best in school. Do everything possible to prevent dropping out.
- Help your kids identify positive role models and heroes—especially people right in your community.
- Do everything possible to involve your children in supervised, positive group activities.
- Praise your children for doing well and encourage them to do their very best—to stretch their skills to the utmost.
- Know what your children are doing and whom they are with. Know about their friends and their friends' families.

You can best serve as the first line of defense against gangs by participating actively in community, civic, and social activities that strengthen the family structure and give your children healthy alternatives to gang involvement. You can't say, "Don't look to those people for your needs," without having anything else to offer. For referrals to alternative programs in your area or for expert advice on how to keep kids out of gangs, you can contact Nelson Baez Associates (see Resources).

RESOURCES

National Crime Prevention Council
1700 K Street N.W., 2nd floor
Washington, DC 20006
(202) 466-6272

National Youth Gang Center Institute
for Intergovernmental Research
P.O. Box 12729
Tallahassee, FL 32317
(904) 385-0600, ext. 2449 or 285

Nelson Baez Associates
733 Clinton Avenue
South Plainfield, NJ 07080
(908) 769-1664

FOR FURTHER READING

Especially for Teens
Barden, Renardo. *Gangs*. Vero Beach, Fla.: Rourke Corporation, 1990.

Webb, Margot. *Coping with Street Gangs*. New York: Rosen Publishing Group, 1990.

Homosexuality

Your teens already know about homosexuality. Since grade school they've heard words like *faggot*, *queer*, and *homo* thrown around the school yard. By now they know that these names ridicule homosexuals. They may have discussed the subject in health classes that cover sexuality or diversity in family relationships. They may have sat in your living room and watched actor Ellen DeGeneres come out of the closet on national TV. They probably saw *Friends* character Ross lose his wife to her lesbian lover. And if they're listening to the news, they know all about the controversy over gays in the military or the trial of a gay Boy Scout leader. So you might ask, "What's to talk about?"

Plenty! These bits and pieces of information may have come together in a confusing mess of misconceptions. And even if your child's school has given out the facts, it hasn't explained how you feel about the subject and how you would react if your child said, "I think I'm homosexual." You need to talk.

HOW DO YOU FEEL
ABOUT HOMOSEXUALITY?

Before you broach this subject with your teen, stop and think about your own feelings. If you are a straight parent with negative opinions about homosexuality, it's very important that you make an effort to explore your feelings on this subject before you talk with your teens. It's not the intent of this chapter to change your beliefs, but it is our hope that we can encourage you to allow your children a more tolerant attitude. They will live, work, and associate with male and female homosexuals throughout their lives; some of them will grow to discover their own homosexual orientation. Their adult years will be more peaceful and productive if they are not encumbered with homophobic feelings.

If you have strong feelings against homosexuality, take a moment to consider why you feel this way. Many of the old beliefs that may have influenced you are changing. In 1973, for example, the American Psychiatric Association removed homosexuality from its list of psychological disorders, and in 1975, the American Psychological Association began an aggressive campaign to remove the label of mental illness from homosexuality. So it is not, as you might have been taught, a psychological illness. Also, most religions are currently changing their traditional policy of condemning homosexuality, instead now defining homosexuals as "persons of sacred worth." In a recent pastoral letter titled "Always Our Children," the Roman Catholic bishops in the United States advise parents of gay children to love and support their sons and daughters. The bishops say homosexual orientation is not freely chosen and that parents must not reject their gay children in a society full of rejection and discrimination. Perhaps your views of homosexuality as deviant or immoral have not kept up with these changes. Whatever your feelings, it is to your teen's benefit to convey a tolerant, unemotional, and matter-of-fact view of homosexuality.

If you are a straight parent who has an unprejudiced outlook, you will be able to talk to your teens about homosexuality without intentional bias. However, you too should check your attitude before you speak. Many well-intentioned straight people express pity for the sexual orientation itself, rather than outrage for the prejudice it attracts. For example, it's important not to present homosexuality as a "problem" some people have. You also want to be careful not to emphasize the societal difficulties experienced by the "poor" homosexual. Homosexuals don't want anyone's pity; they need matter-of-fact acceptance as human beings.

If you are a gay parent, you most certainly have a need to talk directly with your children about homosexuality. However, you'll find that because most parents and therefore most of our readers are not gay, the information offered here may not address your circumstance exactly. Still, you will surely find some words that will help you answer the inevitable questions your teens will ask.

WHY TALK ABOUT HOMOSEXUALITY?

Teens are overwhelmingly curious about their own identity as males and females and about whether their emerging sexuality will be accepted by their peers. If they pick up the silent signal that homosexuality is a taboo subject, they will assume it is "bad" and open to cruel ridicule. Strong prejudices against homosexuals (rooted in fear) begin in the teen years with vicious taunting. This attitude

perpetuates the problem of homophobia in this country. You can
have a hand in creating a more tolerant and accepting world of
tomorrow by talking to your teens today.

During the early teens, some young people experiment sexually with friends of the same sex and become worried that they
might be homosexual. They need to know that this is a subject that
can be talked about. Once the subject is open to discussion, they
can receive the needed reassurance that early experimentation does
not cause homosexuality (see the following information about talking to teens under age fifteen).

Despite their claim to know all about homosexuals, many
teens live with major misconceptions. They assume that all "fags"
talk and walk funny. They may think gay people try to convert
straight people. They stereotype lesbians as she-man "dykes." They
need someone to explain the very human, everyday, normal side of
homosexual people.

If your teen is grappling with homosexual tendencies, he or
she needs to know you are a person who will listen. Your honest,
candid approach to the subject will help him or her avoid becoming one of the disproportionately high numbers of gay, lesbian, bisexual, and transgender youth caught up in depression, substance use,
homelessness, and suicide. A study released in 1998 by the Harvard
Medical School found that gay and bisexual teenagers engage in
more risky behaviors than their heterosexual peers. Those risks
included having sex before age thirteen, engaging in unsafe sex, and
using cocaine, alcohol, and marijuana before age thirteen. The
authors said that the gay teenagers most likely to take risks are those
who grow up without support for their sexual orientation, especially
from their family. If your child has concerns about her sexuality, you
want her to know that you are "safe" to talk to.

HOW AND WHEN
TO TALK ABOUT HOMOSEXUALITY

Like reproductive sexuality, homosexuality is not a subject that lends itself to long lectures out of the blue. It is best discussed during teachable moments. Television, radio, and newspapers, for instance, often focus on the issue of homosexuality. When a bulletin focusing on homosexuality (such as gays in the military, in the Boy Scouts, or in the classroom) is broadcast on the TV in your living room or over the radio in your car, grab the opportunity to start a discussion. If you see a gay couple holding hands in the park, don't turn your attention to something else or admonish your teens for being curious with comments like, "Don't stare!" Instead, use the opportunity to talk about what they see. Anytime you find yourself in a teachable moment, you might simply ask, "What do you think about that?" Your teen's response will tell you the direction in which to continue the conversation.

When you talk about homosexuality, talk casually. Don't make this a lecture. Don't get emotional. Relax and have a conversation. This attitude says more than your words. It says that you are open to talking about anything—even the difficult subjects. Also talk directly. Don't beat around the bush. Don't let your own embarrassment or fears interfere with the message you want to give. And talk giving age-appropriate information; a young teen and an older teen may have different concerns about homosexuality (see later in this chapter).

When you talk to your teens about homosexuality, you should make sure you're both talking about the same thing. Take a minute to go over the definitions of the words we use when discussing this subject:

Homosexual: a person who is physically and emotionally
   attracted to people of the same sex
Heterosexual: a person who is physically and emotionally
   attracted to people of the opposite sex
Gay: slang for "homosexual"
Lesbian: a female homosexual
Transgender: a person who feels that he or she is of the opposite
   gender and who takes on the identity of that gender
GLTB: gay, lesbian, transgender, or bisexual
Homophobia: extreme or irrational fear of homosexuals

WHAT TO SAY ABOUT HOMOSEXUALITY

Your teens probably have lots of questions about homosexuality. The
questions that follow are an example of what your teens might ask
you or are silently wondering about.

Teen question: "Why are some people homosexual?
Your response: "Nobody knows for sure why people are gay. Some sci-
entists think that people are born either homosexual or heterosexual. Others think that certain things happen in a person's life that
lead to a homosexual preference. Either way, it's not something that
a person should be blamed for."

Teen question: "Are many people homosexual?"
Your response: "It's estimated that about 10 percent of the population
is gay. That means in America, about twenty-five million people."

Teen question: "Are homosexuals normal?"
Your response: "Yes. Homosexuality is an alternate lifestyle; it is not
a sign of mental illness. Unfortunately, many people hold on to the

old view that gay people are mentally unbalanced. Research shows us that gays (if not persecuted) have no more psychological problems than heterosexuals."

Teen question: "Why do people make fun of homosexuals?"
Your response: "Most of the population is heterosexual. People tend to be afraid of things they don't understand, and sometimes they deal with that fear by putting down anyone who's different from themselves. That's why many homosexuals don't tell anyone who they really are. They're afraid of the ridicule and isolation."

Teen question: "Are homosexuals different from everybody else?"
Your response: "The only thing that makes gay people different is their sexual preference. Other than that, they think and feel exactly like everyone else. They love their families, they want to have friends, they have plans for their future—just like any other person."

Teen question: "Why would anybody want to be homosexual?"
Your response: "Homosexuality isn't something people choose. It is simply who they are. If people had a choice, there would probably be no gay people at all because society makes it so hard to be gay."

Teen question: "When do you know if you're gay?"
Your response: "That's a very individual thing. I can tell you that it's been reported that many gay men and lesbians sensed something 'different' about themselves as early as age four or five. There is a study that says that the age at which most acknowledge their homosexuality is between fourteen and sixteen years for males and between sixteen and nineteen years for females. But these are just averages; everybody is different."

Teen question: "I feel bad when my friends mock this kid in school because he's gay. What should I do?"

Your response: "You're right to feel that no one should be ridiculed because of who they are. You also know that it takes courage to stand up for what you know is right. If you feel strongly about this, you should take a stand. You can interrupt antigay comments and jokes and tell your friends that these things are unfair, offensive, and harmful."

WHAT TO SAY IF YOUR TEEN IS HOMOPHOBIC

Your teen may already have very strong negative feelings about homosexuals. These feelings are based in fear: a personal fear (I need to be sure of my own heterosexuality), a fear of ridicule (I need for my friends to know I'm straight), a fear of things different (They're "queers," and I hate them). You will not change your teen's mind by giving a lecture on tolerance. Homophobic feelings can be very strong and are heavy baggage to carry around. You need to get your teen talking about these feelings before you shut him or her down by saying, "You're wrong." Feelings aren't wrong—they just are.

If your teen makes a comment that makes you suspect homophobia, ask for more information about the feelings behind the comment. Don't be judgmental; just ask questions that will allow a dialogue to start. Ask probing questions like these:

"What makes you say that?"
"Do you know any gay people?"
"Why do you dislike gay people?"

After you have listened without judgment to your teen's opinions, then it's time to offer your own—not as a debate, just another side. You can tell your teen that you have different feelings. You might say that you see homosexuals as human beings, as people who have a lot to contribute to the world. You might even name a few gay people who have attained world admiration. (A few of these people are identified later in this chapter.)

In this kind of nonconfrontational discussion, your teen will learn a lot. He will learn that it's OK to disagree with you. He'll learn that his feelings are not universal. He'll learn that there may be a reason to reconsider his beliefs. You won't convert anyone with one discussion, but you open the door to new ideas.

WHAT TO SAY IF YOUR TEEN "COMES OUT" TO YOU

If your teen blurts out that he or she is a homosexual, our best advice is, Don't react immediately. Take a deep breath and get a better grip on the situation. Your first response will depend on the age of your teen.

Talking to Teens Age Fifteen and Under

If your child is under the age of fifteen, you'll need to give her room to talk and get out her beliefs and fears. Let her cry if she wants; let her tell you all about her feelings. Then, without denying any of her feelings, encourage her to avoid labeling herself just yet. Tell your teen:

"Same-sex attractions may not be a sign of homosexuality. I've read that because young teens are experiencing strong sexual urges at a time when they may not be comfortable even talking with members of the opposite sex, they may unconsciously feel more comfortable directing those feelings toward a member of the same sex. Experts say that for most kids this is a phase of development they will out-grow and that they will eventually form steady relationships with people of the opposite sex. A few early homosexual experiences don't make a person a homosexual."

If you want to throw in a statistic to back up this claim, you can tell your child that researchers at the Harvard School of Public Health and the Center for Health Policy Studies in Washington found that 20.8 percent of American men and 17.8 percent of women surveyed reported homosexual behavior or attraction since age fifteen. Considering that only about 10 percent of the popula-tion is homosexual, these numbers show that many heterosexuals experiment with a same-sex relationships.

Before you end the conversation, tell your child how pleased you are that she felt comfortable confiding in you. Assure her that you love her no matter what her sexual preference. And if she con-tinues to have concerns, you'll talk again any time she likes.

This calm, rational response to what may be an emotional cri-sis to your child will help her deal better with her concerns about emerging sexuality.

Talking to Teens over Fifteen

When an older teen tells his or her parents about feelings of homo-sexuality, the issue should be taken very seriously. At this age, the teen may have already spent years worrying and wondering. This moment of confession was a long time coming and should be han-dled with sensitivity and care. Certainly, some older teens are still confused about their sexual orientation and need time to realize that their feelings for same-sex individuals are a natural part of growing up and no indication of their actual sexual identification. But now, you also have to consider the possibility that your child may be gay or lesbian.

It is very common for parents to react with guilt and anger when faced with their children's homosexuality. Many attempt to deny that the child is really homosexual or try to find someone or something to blame (often themselves). Unfortunately, half of all lesbian and gay youths interviewed reported that their parents rejected them due to their sexual orientation. Don't let this happen in your home. Children should not be rejected for who they are.

As you think about what you should say to your teen, keep in mind that people don't choose their sexual preference and can't be talked out of it. Consider these facts compiled by the Hetrick-Martin Institute that illustrate the strong biological root of homosexuality:

- In a study of 161 homosexual males with twin or adoptive brothers, 52 percent of the subjects' identical twin brothers, 22 percent of their fraternal twin brothers, and 11 percent of their adoptive brothers were homosexual. This supports the theory of a biological link.
- A study of lesbian twin sisters found similar results: the identical twins of lesbians were three times as likely to be lesbian or bisexual than their fraternal twins.
- In a study comparing the brain tissue of nineteen homosexual and sixteen heterosexual men, there was a significant size difference between the two groups in a cluster of cells in the hypothalamus (a region of the brain involved in sexual response).

- In a study of 979 homosexual and 477 heterosexual men, most said that their sexual orientation was established before adolescence.

We offer the following as guidelines to help you know what to say to help your teen.

Express Your Love. Regardless of sexual orientation, your child is still the wonderful person you have loved and have been proud of for so many years. Your unconditional love will provide a safe harbor for your child to discover her true identity and will secure the bond between you. Because it is not easy for a homosexual to live in society, your child needs your love and acceptance more than ever. Closeness to their family is very important for homosexuals. Because most homosexuals do not raise families of their own, they need to maintain strong ties to their parents and relatives. Assure your teen that he is still loved and will be treated the same by you no matter what sexual choices he makes. "I will always love you" is the most powerful response you can give your child.

Be Understanding. You may not understand your child's feelings about his sexual preferences, but you should not ridicule, blame, moralize, or yell at your child or make him feel different because of his sexual orientation. A true dialogue requires listening to your child and trying to understand what he is thinking and feeling. (There is no danger that an understanding attitude will encourage homosexuality. Sexual preference cannot be created through dialogue.) You can help your teen sort out feelings (and increase your own understanding of the situation) by asking questions like these:

"What do you mean by 'gay'?"

"Do all your sexual fantasies center on the same sex?"

"Are you ever attracted to members of the opposite sex?"

"How do you feel about your sexual preference?"

"Did you know that these feelings of attraction toward someone of the same sex are very normal for a person who is gay?"

Offer Counseling. Your teenager is likely to be very willing to
discuss these issues with you openly and honestly if you show tolerance and a desire to understand. Although this is a major step in the
right direction, some teens will still need professional help, especially if they are experiencing "homosexual panic." Psychotherapy
can help a confused or anxious person explore the roots of her sexual identity, her feelings, and her relationships and eventually gain
self-acceptance. (Psychotherapy cannot change one's natural sexual orientation.)

Be Honest. If you're upset about your teen's sexual orientation,
be honest about your feelings, but don't judge your child and insist
that your view is the only right one. This leads to bitter arguments
and may result in an estrangement that can last a lifetime. Instead,
focus on your feelings. Because of the stigma our society still attaches
to homosexuality, you might feel sad about this revelation. Underlying
the sadness will probably be your fear that the child's life may often
be lonely and sad because it deviates from what most people think
adult relationships should be like. You can admit, "I'm upset, but I still
love you." You may feel guilt, or you may mourn the loss of dreams
about grandchildren. Talk about these feelings, but do not hold your
child responsible for them. You own these feelings, and you must deal
with them without blaming your child or passing on the guilt.

Be Tolerant. You can't change your thoughts and feelings overnight, but while you're dealing with your own emotions, try to remain tolerant. Without family support, homosexual teens have nowhere to turn. Students at the Hetrick-Martin Institute in New York (an alternative public school for GLTBs) attest that life is difficult enough for young gay people without losing the love of their parents. These students say they have been physically attacked by their schoolmates and even taunted by their teachers. They had lost their friends, their desire to go to school, and their self-esteem. Their stories are supported by a study reported in the *Journal of Homosexuality*, which found that 80 percent of lesbian, gay, and bisexual youth report severe isolation problems. They experience social isolation (because they have no one to talk to), emotional isolation (because they feel distanced from family and peers), and cognitive isolation (because they lack access to good information about sexual orientation and homosexuality). Home, at least, should be a safe haven, free from censure, a place where your teen can come to terms with who he or she is.

Reach Out. Don't try to handle this alone. Libraries and bookstores are full of information that will help you understand what your teen is going through and how you can help. There are also organizations that give support to gay teens and their families. (See Resources and For Further Reading at the end of this chapter.) Reach out to the sources that can help you.

Offer Hope. Homosexuals are human beings who have much to give to the world and to others. If your teen is gay, you can help him or her see that life holds the same promise that it did before the awareness of sexual orientation. You should educate yourself about lesbian and gay people who have made significant contributions and share them with your teen. Just for starters, historically famous homosexual or bisexual people include Socrates, Leonardo da Vinci, Michelangelo, Walt Whitman, Herman Melville, Tennessee Williams, George Washington Carver, and Leonard Bernstein. Numerous film stars and award-winning athletes have been homosexual or bisexual. Share this information with your teen—it's very hard for gay teens to feel positive and hopeful about their future when their peers make fun of them. Give them a reason to look ahead with hope.

Whether your teen is straight or gay, let him or her know that homosexuality isn't a good or bad thing—it's a sexual orientation that has nothing to do with the person's value as a human being. This attitude prepares your children to live peacefully with all different kinds of people in this world.

RESOURCES

Parents, Families and Friends of Lesbians and Gays (PFLAG)
1101 14th Street N.W., Suite 1030
Washington, DC 20005
(202) 638-4200, ext. 213
Web site: http://www.pflag.org

This organization promotes the health and well-being of gay, lesbian, and bisexual persons and their families and friends. Founded in 1981, PFLAG is now organized in four hundred communities in every state, with sixty-five thousand household members.

Hetrick-Martin Institute
2 Astor Place
New York, NY 10003
(212) 674-2400

Social service, education, and advocacy organization for lesbian,
gay, bisexual, and transgender youth, homeless and runaway
youth, and youth with HIV.

National Youth Advocacy Coalition (NYAC)
1711 Connecticut Avenue N.W., Suite 206
Washington, DC 20009
(202) 319-7596

Coalition of more than one hundred organizations working
together to end discrimination against lesbian, gay, bisexual,
and transgender youth to ensure their physical and emotional
well-being.

National Gay and Lesbian Task Force Policy Institute
1734 14th Street N.W.
Washington, DC 20005

FOR FURTHER READING

Cowan, Thomas. *Gay Men and Women Who Enriched the World*. New
Canaan, Conn.: Mulvey, 1988.

Especially for Teens
Dunbar, Robert. *Homosexuality*. Springfield, N.J.: Enslow, 1995.

Pollack, Rachel, and Cheryl Schwartz. *Journey Out: A Guide for and About Lesbian, Gay, and Bisexual Teens*. New York: Viking Children's Books, 1995.

Sutton, Roger, and Lisa Ebright. *Hearing Us Out: Voices from the Gay and Lesbian Community*. New York: Little, Brown, 1997.

Pornography

Fifteen-year-old Trish was doing research for a school report on HIV/AIDS. She gathered books from the library; she interviewed her uncle who was a doctor, and she checked out the World Wide Web. Knowing that homosexuals are at high risk for acquiring HIV, Trish thought she'd try a search on the Internet using the term *homosexual men*. Within seconds, Trish was offered an international array of 4,260 sites with shockingly vulgar names. She sat staring at color photos of men involved in sex acts she had never imagined. She knew she had stumbled into something her parents wouldn't approve of, but curiosity made it too hard to turn off the computer.

Our teens live in a world where there is easy access to sexually explicit material in magazine and books and on television, movies, videos, and the Internet. It's virtually impossible to shield teens from all forms of pornography because it is as close as a click of the mouse. But it is possible to be vigilant in our efforts to keep pornography out of our homes and to help our children understand its deviant and abnormal nature. It is a fact that pornography can be quite harmful to a teen's developing sexuality if it is viewed without explanation, yet a Canadian study found adolescents using pornography more than adults. Kids like Trish should know that they can talk to their parents about the pornographic materials that litter our world. They will know this if we broach the subject first and give them the go-ahead to ask us questions on this sensitive subject.

TALK ABOUT THE CHANGING FACE OF PORNOGRAPHY

It's important to understand the changing face of pornography. Explicit material is no longer limited to the girly magazines a fifteen-year-old might keep under the bed. Today the trend in pornography is toward portrayals of sexual violence, degradation, and humiliation rather than nudity. Common themes include sadism, incest, child molestation, rape, and even murder. The humor in magazines like *Playboy* focuses on jokes about women drugged (or gotten drunk) and then raped, about gang rape, about castration, about adultery, and even about women and children being tortured or sacrificially murdered. For example, in her book *"Soft Porn" Plays Hardball*, Dr. Judith Reisman describes such a cartoon, in which the reader sees Snow White smiling, trustfully asleep in her little bed. All seven dwarfs are standing alongside her bed while one dwarf calls for a vote: "All in favor of a gang bang, say, 'hi, ho!'" This is what readers are being told is fun and entertaining.

These forms of pornography affect children's attitudes about sex in several ways. They show sex as depersonalized and reduced to a mechanistic function devoid of any feelings. They portray sex without dignity, respect, and love. Pornography glorifies hedonism and self-centeredness rather than love, tenderness, and commitment. It suggests that there is nothing out of the ordinary about sexually brutalizing other people, especially women and children. Aggressive sex is portrayed as normal and exciting.

These are not abstract values. Studies have shown a distinct correlation between the rise in both pornography sales and crimes of sexual violence between the early 1980s and the 1990s. Unfortunately, teenagers, who are basically naive and impressionable, often turn to pornography to find out how to have sexual relations. What they learn is that "everybody" is enjoying disease-free, unproblematic anal, oral, and genital contact with promiscuous, multiple partners. They assume that acts of sexual violence and degradation are normal, common, and harmless.

TALK ABOUT NUDITY

It won't be hard to find opportunities to talk about nudity in the media. Very near nude is the norm in everything from broadcast TV to MTV to city bus ads. It's best to start a discussion with a positive comment about the human body. You might say, "Yes, the [female or male] body is very beautiful." Remind your kids that the great art museums are filled with portraits and sculptures of nude bodies. Then explain:

"However, when the nudity is publicly presented only for sexual arousal—which is a private and personal matter—then it's called pornography. Pornography is not meant for young people. In fact, it's against the law to sell pornographic material to minors. This isn't something that's 'just for fun'; it's trash and it's against the law."

TALK ABOUT INTERCOURSE

When you hear about a magazine, movie, or video with graphic sex, use the opportunity to talk to your teens about the difference between sexual intercourse in real life and pornographic depictions of it. Tell your teens that although sexual intercourse is a perfectly normal act, what these pictures (or movie scenes) depict is deemed pornography because they lack the most important elements of the human sex act: emotion. This kind of pornography suggests that intercourse is impersonal and devoid of love and compassion—it is not.

Teens have no guidelines for judging what's right or wrong in this area, so teach them what you believe. Tell them:

"Pornography takes something that is gentle and beautiful and turns it into something ugly and degrading. One of the things that separates us from the animals is that we don't have intercourse in public. The people who do this are not engaging in the kind of loving relationship that you will want to have when you fall in love."

Then let your kids know that sex itself isn't an off-limits subject. Say:

"I'd be glad to answer any questions you might have about sexual intercourse, or if you'd prefer, I can find you some well-written books on the subject, but it's very important that you understand that what's good and pleasurable about human sexuality is not what's portrayed in pornographic materials."

If your teens get hold of pornography that depicts what we'll call "normal" sexual acts, your goal is to explain that although men and women do have beautiful bodies, and the act of intercourse is a very natural and universal activity, they should not be displayed for the entertainment of others. This message should be delivered without anger; it's a lesson that's intended to help young people put human sexuality in its appropriate perspective—not heap on the guilt.

TALK ABOUT CHILD PORNOGRAPHY, BESTIALITY, AND VIOLENT SEX

You will need to take a very different approach when you talk about "abnormal" acts, such as child pornography, bestiality, or violent sexual acts. In these cases, teens need to be told very firmly that this is not what sex is all about.

This kind of pornography is especially dangerous to the developing morality of teenagers. It gives a false impression of the way normal, civilized men and women engage in sexual activity. It can also interfere with a child's ability to develop a healthy sexual attitude because it offers sexually deviant people as models of behavior and emphasizes perversity and cruelty as norms. If you find your children with this kind of pornographic material, they must be told in no uncertain terms that this is not normal or acceptable.

When you hear about an instance of this kind of pornography on the news or in videos or musical lyrics, use the opportunity to talk about it. Without anger or blame, but still with a no-nonsense demeanor, tell your children that this kind of pornography is pure trash. It is the work of unbalanced people who enjoy hurting others. Tell your teens:

"This is not a healthy way to express sexual feelings. I don't believe that this is the kind of sexual activity you will ever be a part of, so you shouldn't spend time looking at such garbage."

If you find this kind of pornography in your teens' possession, don't explode. Talk about it and assure them that you are not angry. Because you had never spoken about this subject before, you can't punish them for their curiosity (even though they certainly had an inkling that this wasn't material you'd approve of). But let them know that if they spend time with pornographic material again in the future, you will be very angry and will indeed punish their disobedience.

KEEPING PORNOGRAPHY OUT OF YOUR HOUSE

Dr. C. Everett Koop, former U.S. surgeon general, declared pornography a "crushing public health problem," " a clear and present danger," and "blatantly anti-human." "We must oppose it," he says, "as we oppose all violence and prejudice." If you agree, you can take some control over the availability of pornographic material that comes into your home. You can start by purchasing a key for your cable television box. This key, which most cable companies rent by the month, allows you to lock a cable station so no one can view it without your permission.

You can ensure that no one in your home uses telephone "dial-a-porn" services. Just call your business operator and request that outgoing 900 calls be blocked from your phone line.

You can also join the fight against mail-order pornography. Go to your post office and ask for Form 2201. Follow the instructions and record your name and the names of your children under the age of nineteen. They will be added to the Sexually Oriented Advertising (SOA) Prohibitory Reference List, which the Postal Service makes available to mailers.

If you or your children receive a sexually explicit advertisement thirty days of more after your name has been added to the SOA Prohibitory Reference List, take it to the post office for further action. For a first offense, the sender is liable for a fine of up to $5,000 or up to five years in prison or both. Subsequent offenses are punishable by a fine of up to $10,000 or up to ten years in prison or both. This listing terminates five years after the date your name is placed on the list or if you move. If you wish to be kept on the list, you'll need to fill out a new application at that time.

Don't overlook your computer as a source of incoming pornography. There are a number of ways you can block computer access to certain kinds of subjects. Some major Internet access providers, such as America Online and CompuServe, allow parents to customize restrictions by blocking access to sites whose names include words you want to avoid, such as *sex* or *bestiality*. (See "Dangers on the World Wide Web" for more information.)

The experience of viewing pornographic material without parental explanation can harm teenagers both physically and emotionally. To protect them from this experience, we should make a concerted effort to keep pornographic material out of our homes, and we should help children understand that pornography is an abnormal and deviant portrayal of human sexuality.

FOR FURTHER READING

Especially for Teens
Gottfried, Ted. *Pornography: Debating the Issues*. Springfield, N.J.: Enslow, 1997.

Prejudice

The Anderson family lives in a small, close-knit town where everyone knows each other and back doors are never locked. Peg and Ron had raised their two children to be kind and charitable to others and thought they had done a good job, until one Saturday afternoon when they overheard their teens' conversation:

"I don't like Asians or Jews," said Sherry.

"Yeah," agreed Chad. "Asians think they're so smart, and they make it hard for everybody else to get into college. And Jews too; they're always so pushy."

Peg and Ron couldn't imagine where their kids had picked up these opinions and judgments. More upsetting was the question of how their children could have become so prejudiced right under their noses. Was this the way their friends talked? Did they get this idea from TV or movies? What should they do now?

PREJUDICE IN AMERICA

So often, as parents, we are helpless to change the world our children live and grow in. But the issue of prejudice gives us a clear opportunity to have a solid impact on our children and their world—if we choose to speak out, address the problem, and give our kids the information they need to understand and deal with the problem.

We are just beginning to get a clear picture of the consequence of prejudice in America now that the Hate Crimes Statistics Act (passed in 1990) requires the attorney general to collect data on hate crimes. The statistics being gathered are upsetting not only for their volume but also because they are rising each year and because so many hate crimes are committed by teenagers. (Of those arrested for hate crimes in one given year in New York City, 70 percent were under the age of nineteen.)

Although the Civil Rights Act of 1964 declared all people equal under the law regardless of sex, race, color, religion, or national origin, there are still many citizens who focus on differences and use these differences to ridicule, hurt, and attack others. Sadly, these attitudes can be passed through families from generation to generation. In the teen years, when children are so readily influenced by their peers, children from prejudiced families pass their learned biases on to their friends. That's why it is so important to give our teens a foundation in tolerance and to let them know that prejudiced ideas and actions are unacceptable in a democratic society.

THE VOCABULARY OF HATRED

When you talk to your teenagers about prejudice, clarify for them the words that get thrown around when talking about this issue. The following definitions will give you a good place to start.

Bias Incident. Any action a person commits against another person because of having a prejudice or making a prejudgment based on race or ethnicity, sex, religion, age, occupation, social class, sexual orientation, or any number of other categories.
Example: Beating up a person solely because of his or her sexual orientation or race is a bias incident.

Bigotry. The practice of holding to beliefs and opinions in spite of evidence to the contrary.
Example: A person who insists that all women are intellectually inferior to men and won't listen to any other facts or opinions is practicing bigotry. This person is called a *bigot.*

Discrimination. The act or policy of treating someone differently or denying them their rights simply because they belong to a particular group of people.
Example: A firm that hires only a certain race of people is practicing discrimination against all other races and ethnic groups. This is illegal.

Prejudice. To prejudge and to form an opinion without valid information or facts, causing some to fear and be intolerant of others who do not belong to the same ethnic group, religion, gender, and so on.
Example: If you are walking along the sidewalk and, fearing danger, move to the other side of the street when you see a person of a particular race up ahead, you are showing prejudice.

Stereotype. A specialized and oversimplified idea about a whole group of people.
Example: "All guys with long hair are into drugs."

Scapegoating. Blaming an individual or a group when the fault actually lies elsewhere.

Example: Believing an entire race of people is responsible for high college standards or all our social ills.

GIVE CONCRETE EXAMPLES OF PREJUDICE

Racial prejudices are one type of prejudice that all teens are familiar with and are most often sensitive to. But they need to know that there are many other kinds of prejudice that also must be understood and avoided. In your family discussions, give your teens concrete examples of the many kinds of prejudice in the world.

Racial

Extreme examples: Before the civil rights laws of the 1960s, African Americans were not allowed to drink from "white" water fountains, and African American baseball players were not allowed to sleep in the same hotel as their white teammates. In 1997, an American Airlines pilot training guide characterized Latin American passengers as frequently drunk and unruly. Racial prejudice is practiced by the Ku Klux Klan and other white supremacist groups who violently oppose nonwhite Americans.

Everyday examples: People who refuse to sell their homes to people of another race and people who won't shop in a store owned and run by people of a certain race are practicing racial prejudice.

Cultural

Extreme examples: Running native American Indians off their land because new American settlers wanted to live there was cultural prejudice.

Everyday examples: Portraying all Indians as savage warriors, making fun of accents and customs of immigrant families, and ridiculing the dress or mannerisms of foreigners is cultural prejudice.

Religious

Extreme examples: The Holocaust during World War II, which killed thousands of Jewish people, is a well-known example of religious prejudice.

Everyday examples: Ridiculing the religious headdress worn by some Jewish boys or Muslim girls in school shows ignorance and religious prejudice.

Sexism

Extreme examples: Denying women the right to vote until 1920 and refusing to allow women to join certain all-male clubs today are signs of sexism.

Everyday examples: Telling a male athlete that he "runs like a girl" or using forms of the pronoun "he" to refer to all people, as in "Every student should bring *his* book to class," are the kinds of sexism that occur every day.

Sexual Orientation

Extreme examples: Bumper stickers that say "Kill a queer for Christ" advertise the kind of prejudice that caused the 1997 firing of a lesbian lawyer from a law firm after she announced her "marriage" to another woman and the 1997 bombing of a gay and lesbian bar, the Otherside Lounge, in Atlanta, Georgia.

Everyday examples: Homosexuals and lesbians are fired from their jobs, are isolated in communities, are ridiculed in public, and are rejected by their families.

Disabilities

Extreme example: Some stores and companies do not obey the law requiring them to provide convenient facilities for people in wheelchairs to enter and exit buildings and to use drinking fountains, pay telephones, and bathrooms.

Everyday examples: People make fun of others with hearing aids, leg braces, and thick glasses. Children with learning disabilities are ostracized and ridiculed.

Other Forms

- Age and beauty discrimination cause many people embarrassment and pain and also prevent many from finding employment.
- Weight prejudices cause heavy and obese people to be ridiculed and treated as if they were lazy and dumb.
- Diseases, such as AIDS, cause many people to be discriminated against.

HOW TEENS BECOME PREJUDICED

Most teens (like most people) will automatically deny that they are prejudiced. Your conversations on this subject should never include accusations or put your teens on the defensive. Unless you are addressing a specific act of bias committed by your teen, keep the conversation social and talk about the problem in general. Explain:

"All people are exposed to prejudice just by living in and observing a society where prejudices exist. As we grow up we are influenced by many things: TV, music, movies, newspapers, entertainment shows, friends, and family. Sometimes, without even realizing it, we take on beliefs that have no basis in reality. We learn to judge people blindly without even knowing them. We forget to be sensitive to other people's feelings. If we're not on guard against these influences, we can become prejudiced ourselves."

MONITOR YOUR OWN PREJUDICES

You can best convey a nonbiased attitude to your teens if you first take some time to tune into your own prejudices. In truth, most people are prejudiced to some degree. Deep down, do you believe that some ethnic groups are dumb or smart? Or naturally good at sports? Or responsible for social ills? Prejudice is so contagious that we must be extremely vigilant in our words and our actions. Think about your own beliefs before you talk to your children.

Don't Identify People by Race

If your teen wants to invite a friend to your house, but you're not sure which friend she means, don't ask, "Is that the Chinese girl?" Look for another form of identification such as, "Is that the girl with the long, dark hair who played on your soccer team last year?"

Don't Focus Conversation on Racial Differences

When you talk about others you meet at work or in the community, don't let your comments focus on personal attributes. If you have a problem with a family in your neighborhood, for example, don't attribute your conflict to racial, ethnic, class, or religious factors. Talk about the problem you have with that individual—completely isolated from his or her ancestry.

Avoid Ethnic Jokes

Stereotypical ethnic humor is a traditional staple of comedy. However, your example in this matter is most important to your children. It will be very difficult for them to understand why it's OK to poke fun around the dinner table at a "dumb" ethnic group, but it's not acceptable to ridicule a classmate of that ethnic group for being dumb. Teens are very sensitive to any sign of hypocrisy in their parents. Don't leave yourself open to this charge.

Don't Stereotype People

Be careful how you explain why certain people have particular skills, talents, or habits. If, for example, a friend is especially good at soccer, be careful not to attribute that fact to the child's race or nationality. Or, if your child wants to know why a family on your block often has such large family gatherings, don't explain the occurrence based on your understanding of the family's ethnic origin. Instead, always relate exceptional qualities or circumstances to the individual—not to the person's race.

Practice Impartiality

What you do speaks louder than anything you can say to your teens, so teach your beliefs through your actions:

- Do sit next to a family of a different race in the fast-food restaurant.
- Do invite people of different races from the neighborhood or school into your home.
- Do keep a pleasant tone of voice and manner when interacting with strangers of other races in the store, on the bus, or the like.

- Do show your children that the way you act toward people has nothing to do with the way they look.

BUILD UP SELF-ESTEEM

Low self-esteem plays a big role in the development of prejudices. Teens who don't feel secure in their own identity will build themselves up by putting others down. On the other side of the coin, teens with a low self-image have weak psychological defenses against the prejudices of others. Nurturing pride in your teen's accomplishments and abilities will help him or her stand strong against the temptation to act with prejudice and against the hurt of being the victim of prejudice.

Compliment!
It can be a challenge, but you should find at least one good thing to compliment in your teen every day. Comment positively when he wears something nice (or at least something that is a nice color). Compliment any and every attempt at responsible and independent work. Say, "I'm glad to see you working so hard on that homework assignment." Reinforce the goodness of their race, ethnicity, sex, age, and so on. Say, "We're so lucky as [ethnic group] to have such a long and rich history." Say, "You have more advantages and opportunities as a female in this day and age than at any other time in the history of the world." And so on.

Keep in mind that the goal in building a teen's self-esteem is to build pride in self—not to promote a sense of superiority. It would be counterproductive to the cause of teaching tolerance and acceptance if you say, "Don't let that [white, black, Hispanic, Jewish] boy tell you what to do. He just wants to keep you down." Or, "If you study hard you can be even smarter than that [racial group] girl in your class." Or, "You can play basketball as well as any black athlete." Instead, compliment and encourage your kids on what they do as individuals, not as compared to people of other races.

Let Your Kids Know You Love Them
A person is capable of caring about the needs of others only when his or her own need for affection and acceptance is met. Tell your teenagers that you love them. Give them lots of hugs (whether they like it or not). Don't miss an occasion to smile, wink, and give a thumbs-up.

RECOGNIZE AND DISCUSS DIFFERENCES

Teenagers are not color-blind. We can't ask them to pretend that people are not different from each other. We *are* all different in color, shape, beliefs, and experiences—use these differences to teach sensitivity and acceptance.

Use Life Experiences
All around you are daily opportunities to teach your children to accept and enjoy the differences among people. Look for them and use them. For example, if you are not of Indian descent, don't just ignore the Indian man with a turban and a woman with a dot in the center of her forehead when you see them walking down the street (thinking that silence shows tolerance). Talk about it. Ask your teen whether she knows the Indian names for the turban and the dot. Does she know why they wear them? If she doesn't, say, "I think I'm going to go to the library this week and get a book about

India. Let's find out if the turban and dot mean anything specific in their culture."

Turn the Tables

You can also teach tolerance in day-to-day situations by turning the table on your teens. Teens are notorious for complaining that adults judge them based on appearance rather than on their character and abilities. Turn the tables and help teens understand why it's unfair for *anybody* to judge another person based on stereotypes that are picked up from society.

Ask them: "If teens want us to accept their crazy hair and piercings and clothing and music, shouldn't they tolerate diversity too?"
Tell them: "If you always keep in mind how much you dislike being judged by people who don't really know you, you'll be able to resist the temptation to prejudge others."

Use the News and TV

News and TV shows teach all of us a lot about prejudice. Quite often, you'll hear a report of a government official or a CEO or a celebrity making a prejudiced comment (as did Marge Schott, owner of the Cincinnati Reds baseball team, known for her repeated use of racial and ethnic slurs). You'll see news of a race riot (like the one in Los Angeles after the Rodney King verdict was delivered), or a hate crime (like the ones in which teens desecrated Jewish cemeteries by spray painting swastikas on gravestones), or a case of discrimination (like the complaints of airline attendants who charged that age and weight limitations are discriminatory). Jump on these as opportunities to talk. Give your opinion and ask your teens what they think about the event. Ask them to support their view. Find out how they feel.

Television offers daily opportunities for talking about prejudice and stereotypes. It's not uncommon for TV shows to cast Latin Americans as drug dealers, African Americans as teenage hoods, and Native Americans as bloodthirsty savages. When you see these stereotypes on television, point them out, label them as stereotypes, and talk with your kids about them.

RESPOND TO PREJUDICED AND INTOLERANT REMARKS

A not-to-be-missed opportunity to talk about prejudice and tolerance presents itself when you hear someone—perhaps even your own kids—make a racial slur or any other put-down based on a person's religion, sex, or appearance. What would you say to your teen if you heard him or her or some friends make remarks like these:

"What a creep! He's so fat and he wears that stupid hearing aid."
"Don't let her come to the party. [Racial or ethnic group] kids are such a drag."
"I don't care what the teacher says; I'm not sitting next to that [racial slur]."

There are lots of ways you might react, but remember this: don't get angry and don't ignore. Anger makes children defensive and closed to a learning opportunity; ignoring implies acceptance. Instead, keeping a calm tone, ask your children why they feel a person of a different race, religion, or appearance might not make a good friend. Listen to the response.

You might say: "You sound as if you know all the people who are [name of group] and that you don't like any of them. You can only like or dislike people you know. If you don't know someone, you can't have a good reason for liking or not liking them."

Then admit: "There may be kids you don't like to hang out with."

Then teach: "But the reason should have nothing to do with the way they look or the color of their skin."

DEALING WITH DISCRIMINATION

It is very difficult for any parent to hear that their child has been victimized by prejudice. What do you say to a teenager who comes home crying because someone on the bus taunts her with racial slurs? Your response will teach your children a great deal. You can use the circumstance to teach empowerment or you can respond with your own brand of hate and a pledge of revenge. The better choice is obvious but not always easy. You may feel as angry or upset as your child, but try to keep in mind that you have a valuable learning opportunity in front of you—use it wisely.

Don't Overreact

Teenagers can be cruel. A great deal of teasing and bullying goes on all day long. A bias incident may really be a stab at ridicule, rather than a conscious act of prejudice. Before you react, get the facts. Try to keep your own outward distress to a minimum so that you can concentrate on helping your teen. It is fine to share your contempt and revulsion for this kind of behavior, but don't panic or spread more fear and anxiety. Overreactive references to the historic struggles of your people and the atrocities of the past will serve only to add to your child's fears. Focus on your child's feelings and on what you can do together about the incident.

Be Honest

If your child is different from the majority of other children in your community in religion, skin color, or cultural background, nothing is gained by telling him that he is not different or that all people are alike. If the problems caused by differences are not faced, they will form the basis of festering anxieties and self-doubts. Tell your teen:

"Yes, you are different. Human beings differ in their appearance, in the ways they worship God, in their dress, in their dances, songs, and language. These differences are natural and desirable. No human being should ever need to apologize for the fact that he or she is different."

As you know, however, we live in an imperfect society where injustice exists and people can be insensitive and hurtful. Your teen now knows this also. You might try to explain prejudice like this:

"Unfortunately, people *are* treated differently, and often for unimportant reasons. It may be because their skin is a different color, or because they do not have as much money as other people, or because they go to a different church, or because they speak with an accent, or for any other reason. Many people before you have faced this kind of prejudice and discrimination and know how hurtful it is."

Talk About Feelings

Before you can discuss how your teen should handle these situations, take some time to validate and talk about those hurtful feelings. A bias attack makes anyone feel very angry—make sure your teen knows that's normal. Then put the attack in perspective. Say:

"That must have really hurt you. But it is very important that you never let the words of others change how you feel about yourself. You are not to blame when people hate or reject you for things you have no control over. You are not the one with a problem. You are a special and good person. It is people who are prejudiced and full of hate who have the problem. A person who hates others without even knowing them is a victim of ignorance and distortions. Sometimes they need to put down other people just so they can feel superior. Don't let that happen. Don't let them make you feel inferior."

Take Action Against Prejudice

Prejudice is wrong, and it is unfair, and you need to help your teen decide how to handle the situation if it happens again in the future. When confronted with difficult situations like this, people tend to react without thinking. The natural response is to strike back (verbally or physically), but this often makes the situation worse. Another natural reaction is to generalize feelings of ethnic or racial hatred toward the attacker. Let your teen know that these reactions are understandable but that they do nothing to solve the problem or reduce prejudice in the world. Tell your teen that revenge is not the answer, and then show her how she can become part of the solution.

Encourage your teens to turn anger into positive action. Don't let them simmer or sulk—push them to *do* something. Talk to your kids about what to do when they are the victims of a bias attack. Knowing that there are things they can do will take away those feelings of helplessness:

Talk to Someone About It. "Telling a sympathetic person about what happened and how it hurt you will help you feel better. Bias attacks are nothing you should try to hide or should feel embarrassed about. Choose a friend, a teacher, a counselor, or me to go to immediately."

Don't Let a Put-Down Keep You Down. "Take charge, stand up, and hold your head up high. The prejudices of others may make you feel fearful, left out, and disliked. But never forget that you have done nothing wrong, so don't act like you have." (As obvious as it may seem to you, your child needs to hear that there is no truth to what an attacker said.)

Be Assertive, Not Aggressive. "An aggressive response returns the hurt and stupidity of prejudice. But an assertive response helps you feel proud of yourself and does something to change the situation. Your goal is to prevent a fight, stop the cycle of prejudice, and preserve your own sense of pride. If someone calls you a hateful name, don't call that person some other name, and don't start a fight. A dignified response would be to say quietly, 'I'm African American [or other proper name], and I'm proud of that.'"

Get Help. "If the prejudiced person won't leave you alone or threatens to do you harm, get help. Going to an adult is not a sign of weakness or 'tattling,' it is a sign of intelligence. Bias attacks are serious, and they are against the law. Let the people who can help you know what's going on."

Keep Your Head Up. "Don't let anyone's narrow-mindedness keep you from reaching your goals. When someone hassles you or calls you names, you can't let this convince you that you're no good.

Use the anger you feel to push yourself even harder to be the best you can be."

Role-Play
If your teen is having difficulty dealing with prejudice, arm him or her with a sense of confidence that comes from knowing in advance what to do and say.

Offer a few different scenarios:

- Imagine you hear someone at the lunch table say a derogatory remark about your sex, disability, or race loud enough to make sure you can hear.
- Imagine that someone intentionally bumps into you and then angrily calls you a name that ridicules your race.
- Imagine that someone scrawls a prejudiced remark or symbol on your locker.
- Imagine that one person is turning all your friends against you.

Help your teen brainstorm ways to handle these kinds of situations. There is no one perfect or right response; your teen has to decide what makes her feel strong and comfortable. Ask:

"What will happen if you respond with anger and hatred?"
(Remind your teen that this option may further convince narrow-minded people that they're right in putting him down.)
"What will happen if you respond with angry silence?" (Explain the danger of building up one's own internal store of hatred and becoming prejudiced oneself.)
"What will happen if you respond by completely ignoring the bigot?"

"What will happen if you respond by speaking up in a calm manner, explaining that you don't want to hear such bigoted remarks again?"

"What will happen if you walk away?"

"What will happen if you report the incident to a teacher?"

Thinking about the consequences of each response will help your teen decide what course of action to take if he becomes victimized again—this alone will make your teen feel less powerless.

INSTILL PRIDE

Make sure your teens know about their cultural heritage. Talk about the hardships and triumphs of their grandparents. Let them know that you are proud of your roots and ancestors. Spend time as a family exploring. Use encyclopedias. Visit museums. Tour native lands on the Internet. Enjoy old family pictures. If your children know where they come from and have a sense of pride in this background, they'll be better equipped intellectually and emotionally to withstand the hurt of prejudice and discrimination.

RESOURCES

National Hate Hotline
(800) 347-HATE
Report hate crimes to this number.

Anti-Defamation League of B'nai B'rith
823 United Nations Plaza
New York, NY 10017
Web site: http://www.adl.org

National Institute Against Prejudice and Violence
31 South Greene Street
Baltimore, MD 21201
(410) 328-5170

FOR FURTHER READING

National PTA and the Anti-Defamation League of B'nai B'rith. *What to Tell Your Child About Prejudice and Discrimination*. New York: National PTA and the Anti-Defamation League of B'nai B'rith, 1997.

Especially for Teens

Duvall, Lynn. *Respecting Our Differences*. Minneapolis, Minn.: Free Spirit, 1994.

Edwards, Gabrielle. *Coping with Discrimination*. New York: Rosen Publishing Group, 1992.

Kranz, Rachel. *Straight Talk About Prejudice*. New York: Facts on File, 1992.

Puberty

The early signs of puberty quickly litter a young teen's bedroom. You'll see your daughter experimenting with sport bras, makeup, jewelry, and teen-idol magazines. Boys will store away sport bar deodorant, aftershave, combs, and *Playboy* magazine. These possessions are all outward signs of what's going on inside a young teen's body. This is a time when the world changes, feelings change, and even the way the body looks changes. This is definitely a time when your young teen needs to talk to you.

WHAT EXACTLY IS PUBERTY?

Puberty is a period of time when a child reaches sexual maturity and becomes able to reproduce. The onset of puberty is not dictated by a specific age but rather by certain physical and emotional changes that can occur over the course of several years. The process is unique in each child. The first physical sign of puberty in girls usually appears sometime between the ages of nine and thirteen. In boys, it usually appears between ten and fourteen. But no one can say, for example, that all girls should have underarm hair by age fifteen or that boys should have beards at seventeen. Some teens develop all their sex characteristics early and quickly; others mature later and more slowly. Either course (and everything in between) is perfectly normal.

WHO SHOULD DO THE TALKING ABOUT PUBERTY?

Traditionally, moms talk to their daughters about puberty, and dads to their sons. But in the world today, this is not necessarily the way it works—or should work. In two-parent families, one parent may feel more comfortable talking about human growth and development than the other; this is the parent who should talk to the kids, regardless of sex. In single-parent homes, the job is left to the remaining parent, or even to a grandparent or favored aunt or uncle. Who gives the information is not as important as how the information is given. Teens will learn to feel good about their growing bodies if they are given the information they need from an honest, caring, and empathic adult.

WHEN TO TALK ABOUT PUBERTY

Ideally, you have already spoken to your teens about the changes they experience during puberty (because the changes probably began a few years ago). If you have, you'll want to continue these talks as new feelings and physical changes pop up throughout the teen years. But if your teen is sixteen years or older and you haven't yet brought up the subject of puberty, it's probably too late to start the conversation now; jump over to the chapter "Sex, Contraception, and Pregnancy" for information on these topics. If your teen is under sixteen, it's not too late; there is still a lot going on that you can explain and give support to.

There is no one correct time to talk about puberty. In fact, it's better if you don't sit down and give your teen the Big Talk. The changes and concerns of puberty occur over several years. Make it a point to talk to your son or daughter on many occasions throughout the early teen years.

You might use the obvious physical changes that occur during this time as your launching pad. If your teen has a friend who is maturing before the others, talk about it. You might say, "I saw Tom the other day and was surprised to see how mature he's getting. He's got a little moustache growing. Have you noticed it?" Or to your daughter you might comment, "I noticed Kathy is wearing a bra now. Do you think you'll be needing one soon?" These simple and casual comments let your teen know that you're aware that this is a time of change for all young teens.

HOW TO TALK ABOUT PUBERTY

When you talk to your teens about puberty, keep these few tips in mind:

Talk Honestly. If talking about puberty is difficult or embarrassing for you, that's OK. Just say so. Admit to your teen, "This is embarrassing for me to talk about, but I think it's important."

Talk Matter-of-Factly. You can convey the message to your teen that puberty is part of normal, healthy development by speaking often and matter-of-factly about the physical and emotional changes this period brings: "I bought you your own deodorant today; now that you're growing into an adult, you'll sweat more and you'll need this."

Talk Positively. Be sure to paint a very positive picture of puberty. Let your teen know that he or she has a reason to feel glad and proud about reaching this stage of growth: "This is a very exciting time for you; so much will be changing and happening to the way you look and feel."

Talk Seriously. It may be tempting to use humor to handle the changing physical and emotional state of your teen, but it's usually not helpful, and it can be hurtful. Pubescent teens are very sensitive and will often take even the most innocent jest to heart.

Talk Empathically. It's a good idea to ask your teen, "Do you have any questions about puberty?" But you can bet the answer will be no. You might get a better response (eventually) if you follow that up with an anecdote about your own experiences that shows your teen you went through this yourself once and suffered through a number of embarrassing and scary moments.

There's no need to share intensely personal experiences, but it's been known to open the door of communication when a mother admits to her daughter, for example, that she suffered through months of a vaginal infection as a teen because she was too embarrassed to say the word *vagina* to her mother. Or when a father describes his confusion and surprise after experiencing his first wet dream. Just knowing that you know about these things is very reassuring and may help your teen open up about things on his or her mind.

Talk Patiently. When you talk about the changes of puberty, you can expect your teen to turn several shades of red, mumble a few incoherent words, and turn away. Don't throw your hands up and surrender. You can encourage future discussions by simply saying something like, "I know that it can be embarrassing to talk about some parts of puberty because they are signs of your growing sexuality, but I just want you to know that I've been through puberty myself, and I remember feeling confused a lot of times. I didn't know if what I was going through was normal or not. I want you and me to talk about these changes as they happen so you won't have to be concerned or worried."

WHAT TO TALK ABOUT

When you broach the subject of puberty, don't mix up puberty and sex. Discussions about puberty should focus on the physical and emotional changes that occur as your child grows into adulthood. We talk about "teen sex" in "Sex, Contraception, and Pregnancy." But before you jump into discussions about intercourse and contraception, teens need a chance to understand their changing bodies and emotions. They need to know that they can say the word *penis* or *vagina* without embarrassing you or themselves before they can talk to you about intercourse, promiscuity, contraception, and the rest.

TALKING TO BOYS ABOUT PUBERTY

Boys' introduction to puberty begins with slow but sure physical changes that affect their size and appearance. You should first talk to your son about the changes he'll be most acutely aware of. These include the following:

- *Skin*. During puberty, pimples may begin to appear on the face and often on the back. Acne will become a problem for approximately 70 percent of teenagers (especially boys).
- *Chest*. A boy's breasts may get slightly larger and feel tender temporarily. Assure your son that if this happens to him, it is perfectly normal and will soon pass.
- *Voice*. The male voice gets deeper during puberty, but while in transition it may crack or squeak occasionally. Let your son know that this is to be expected and that he should not feel embarrassed when it happens.
- *Body hair*. Alert your son to the fact that he will soon begin growing hair in his genital area, under his arms, perhaps on his chest, and eventually on his face.
- *Sweat glands*. This is the time to emphasize good hygiene and introduce deodorant, because boys will now begin to perspire more.
- *Size*. As your boy grows rapidly in size and weight during puberty, he may find that he temporarily loses some physical coordination and may feel clumsy at times. He should also know that some boys grow early and quickly, others grow later and slowly, and both are perfectly normal.
- *Genitals*. As the male body develops in sexuality, first the scrotum and testicles begin to enlarge. Later the penis itself increases in size.

About one year after the beginning of these changes, boys usually acquire the capacity to produce and ejaculate sperm. This typically occurs as a surprise during masturbation or a wet dream. Your son will accept the bodily changes of puberty in a positive way if you tell him *beforehand* that soon he will be capable of producing and ejaculating sperm.

Your son may be somewhat embarrassed by a discussion of ejaculation, but he will also be relieved to know that he can talk to you about anything during this time of change. Here are some questions you might expect and some suggested answers:

Teen question: "How does an erection happen?"
Your response: "Erections happen when the penis becomes enlarged and firm and stands erect. Like yawning, erections are very normal and often involuntary. They're a natural part of being male. During the teen years, the penis becomes more sensitive, and erections occur more frequently, sometimes for no apparent reason. Although this may be embarrassing, it's normal. Generally, erections occur in three ways: (1) when the male is sexually aroused, blood fills the spongelike tissues in the penis, which causes it to become enlarged; (2) when he is asleep, a male may experience a buildup of semen that will give him an erection; or (3) a bladder full of urine can put pressure on the reproductive organs and cause the penis to become erect. That's why males from infancy through adulthood often wake in the morning with an erection."

Teen question: "What does it mean to 'come'?"
Your response: "When a man is sexually aroused, he can reach a peak of excitement that can end with an orgasm. Having an orgasm is called 'coming.' When a man has an orgasm, his penis muscles contract and relax while a whitish sticky fluid called semen shoots out of the tip in short spurts. This is called ejaculation. Ejaculation can result from sexual stimulation such as masturbation or sexual intercourse. After ejaculation, the penis returns to its normal size."

Teen question: "Why do some boys have large penises and some boys have small ones?"

Your response: "There is no such thing as a 'normal' penis. The size and appearance of external sexual organs are different in every person. Size and shape have nothing to do with sexual pleasure or masculinity."

Teen question: "If I don't come when I have an erection, will I get sick or hurt my penis?"
Your response: "No. If the erection lasts for a long time, you may experience a dull, sensitive, swollen feeling (especially in the testes) when the penis returns to its soft state. This feeling is short-lived, is not harmful, and will not make you sick or injure your penis."

Teen question: "What's a wet dream?"
Your response: "Wet dreams happen when you ejaculate while you're sleeping. They are one way that the male body gets rid of extra sperm, and they are very normal. If you wake in the morning and find you've had a wet dream, just take your sheets off the bed and put them with your pajamas in the laundry [or the washing machine, or whatever]. Don't feel embarrassed. Your mom and I expect this to happen because you're growing up now."

TALKING TO GIRLS ABOUT PUBERTY

Although the female's reproductive organs are primarily hidden inside the body, there are some outer physical changes your daughters will observe during puberty:

- First the hips begin to broaden, and the breasts begin to develop. (Tell your daughters that it's normal for one breast to grow more quickly than the other.)

- Then hair will appear under the armpits and in the genital area.
- Body height increases as much as three inches; hands and feet may seem disproportionately large because they grow faster than the rest of the body. (This is when your daughters may begin to slump over to camouflage the fact that they're taller than the boys.)
- Skin becomes thicker, more oily, and sometimes pimply, and perspiration increases. (This is a good time to put renewed emphasis on personal hygiene.)
- Finally, about two to two-and-a-half years after breast development begins, your daughter will begin menstruation.

Talking About Menstruation

Before your daughter menstruates, let her know what happens in a woman's body each month, and why. Unless your daughter's friends are already talking about menstruation, young girls don't usually ask for this information, so you have to bring up the subject at a time when the two of you are alone and have some uninterrupted time. This is not a time for a lecture but rather a time to open the door to frequent and factual discussions.

The key to establishing a positive, accepting attitude toward menstruation is in the way you prepare your daughter in advance. Shortly after you notice hip and breast development, it's time to talk about the inevitable monthly period.

Rather than begin your talk with an explanation of ovaries and eggs, it's best to begin with the part of menstruation that most overtly affects your daughter—monthly bleeding. Some girls already know about monthly periods from their friends or school lessons, but you will still want to make sure that your child has her facts straight.

Show your daughter tampons and sanitary pads and explain, "These are products that absorb the blood that passes out of a woman's uterus and through the vagina every month. This monthly bleeding is called menstruation. Because you're getting older, you'll soon start menstruating, and I don't want you to be frightened when you see blood. I want you to know it's perfectly normal and a good sign that you're becoming a healthy woman."

Use yourself as a model (if you're a dad, talk about women in general). "Every month, I bleed through my vagina for about four or five days. I put a tampon into my vagina to absorb the blood, and I put a pad in my underwear to catch any blood that seeps out. I change my tampon every few hours."

At this point, your daughter will either ask you why this happens, or they'll tell you they already know about periods. In either case, continue:

"Because you will be getting your monthly period sometime in the near future, I think it's important for you to know why women bleed like this."

At this time, give your daughter the facts. You might want to refer to one of the books suggested at the end of this chapter, or you can give your own knowledgeable explanation. In brief, remember to mention these points:

Females are born with a supply of eggs in their ovaries. Beginning during pubescence, one egg at a time is released approximately every twenty-eight days by one of the ovaries. This egg travels through tubes from the ovary to the uterus. The uterus prepares to receive it by creating a lining composed of blood and other fluids and substances. If the egg is fertilized as a result of sexual intercourse, the egg becomes embedded in this lining, and a baby develops. If the egg is not fertilized, the lining dissolves and is released as menstrual flow through the vagina.

Most important, tell your daughter what to do when she first begins menstruating. Assure her that when she first sees a bit of blood, she need not worry. If she is away from home, she should go to the school nurse or nearest bathroom for a sanitary pad or wad of toilet tissue.

Emphasize the normal aspect of menstruation and encourage your daughter to let you know if she should see any blood or even brown stains on her underwear or on the toilet tissue when she wipes herself after urination.

Here are a few questions you can expect and some suggested answers:

Teen question: "How much blood comes out?"
Your response: "The menstrual discharge is heaviest during the first few days. The total menstrual discharge amounts to about half a cup, but there are only four to six tablespoons of blood. The rest is made up mostly of extra uterine lining, which explains why the discharge is often brownish in color."

Teen question: "Will I be able to go to gym class and play sports?"
Your response: "Menstruation is a normal part of every woman's life, and there's no reason to change any part of your daily schedule at this time. You can shower, dance, run, exercise, swim, and play without worrying."

Teen question: "Will I feel sick?"
Your response: "Most women feel perfectly fine throughout their period. Some do experience some abdominal cramps, but light exercise or a heating pad usually relieves the discomfort. Others feel a

little moody or tense just before their period begins. The reason for this is simple: the female hormones—estrogen and progesterone—that cause the lining of the uterus to thicken usually help keep you calm and upbeat. Just before menstruation begins, the production of these hormones is reduced, resulting in a let-down feeling. This feeling is strictly temporary and disappears as menstruation starts. Some people call this time PMS, for 'premenstrual syndrome.'"

Teen question: "Will I have a period for the rest of my life?"
Your response: "Women do not menstruate during pregnancy, but otherwise they generally have periods every month until they are about fifty years old. The end of menstruation, called menopause, usually occurs between forty-five and fifty-five years of age.

"There are a few factors, such as extreme stress or excessive dieting or exercising, that can interrupt the normal menstrual cycle. If you ever skip a period, be sure to let me know so I can help you find out why."

THE EMOTIONAL SIDE OF PUBERTY

The hormonal boost that causes physical changes during puberty also causes many perfectly normal emotional changes that can confuse young teens and drive you to distraction. Remember this when your teen becomes excessively conscious of his appearance and frets over every hair and article of clothing. Try to keep calm when the opinion of her peers far outweighs yours. Relax when classmates of the opposite sex begin to tie up your phone lines. Be understanding when your teen begins to withdraw and act secretive or lashes out with loud complaints. All of these circumstances offer you an opportunity to talk to your young teens. Don't hesitate to say,

"I understand how you're feeling, and I want you to know that even when we disagree I still love you." Letting them know that you understand the intense emotions they feel and want to find a way to help them feel comfortable with themselves is very important during this time of change and transition.

FOR FURTHER READING

Especially for Teens

Bourgeois, Paulette, and Martin Wolfish. *Changes in You and Me: A Book About Puberty, Mostly for Boys.* Kansas City, Mo.: Andrews & McMeel, 1994.

Madaras, Lynda, and Area Madaras. *My Body, My Self for Boys.* New York: Newmarket Press, 1995.

Madaras, Lynda, and Area Madaras. *My Feelings, My Self: A Growing-Up Guide for Girls.* New York: Newmarket Press, 1993.

Violence

In 1998, all the newspapers and TV shows shouted the horrific details of the student rampage in Jonesboro, Arkansas. Sixteen-year-old Renee watched the chief of police on the news break down in tears as he explained that a thirteen-year-old and his eleven-year-old cousin allegedly pulled the fire alarm and then waited on a hill near the school as the students filed out into the parking lot. It was believed that the boys, using hunting rifles with scopes, shot down four of their classmates and one teacher. The very next day, Renee's school had a fire drill, and with a frightened giggle Renee admitted to her mom, "I got really scared when we went outside. I kept looking around for somebody with a rifle."

On hearing this story, we felt bad for children like Renee—they live with fears that are similar to those experienced by children in war-torn countries. Maybe we *are* at war. Anyone who has a radio, a TV, a video game, a CD player, or a ticket to the movies is well aware that we live in a violent society. And maybe it's time for all of us to pick a side: for or against violence. Having an open discussion with your teenager about the effects of violence may help you both to choose wisely.

WHY TALK ABOUT VIOLENCE

We need to talk to our teens about violence because, unfortunately, teenagers and young adults are more likely to become victims of violent crimes than any other age segment of the population. This fact affects all our teens, because violence is no longer an inner-city problem that can be excused by blaming the harsh effects of poverty and dysfunctional families. Moral poverty leading to teen violence is now everybody's problem in every town in the country. The statistics are startling:

- In 1996, about a third of all victims of violent crime were ages twelve to nineteen.
- Almost half of all victims of violence were under age twenty-five (although this group makes up less than a quarter of the U.S. population age twelve or older).
- On average each year from 1992 to 1994, about one in fifty persons fell victim to a serious violent crime; among persons age twelve to twenty-four, that number jumped to one in twenty-three.
- The fourteen- to seventeen-year-old age group has supplanted eighteen- to twenty-four-year-olds as the most crime-prone.

News headlines also tell us that younger and younger kids are committing more and more of the serious violent crimes. They seem to be showing more cruelty without remorse. This is a problem that foreshadows a brutal future society that will not be kind to our children if the trend continues.

We believe that the solution is not in increased police patrols or tougher criminal penalties. The long-term answer is right in our homes—all of us have a role to play in teaching our children that violence is wrong. To do this, we have to talk about violence. We have to help our kids recognize that violence is not entertainment (despite the messages to the contrary from the media). We have to talk about nonviolent solutions to everyday problems. We have to talk about the reality of our violent society and how to avoid being victimized. There is a lot to talk about.

WHAT TO DO BEFORE YOU TALK

Adolescents abhor hypocrisy. If you expect to convince your kids that violence is not an acceptable solution to life's problems, you need to take a close look at how you resolve your own conflicts. Kids need to grow up seeing people deal with their anger. They need to learn that although anger is natural, it can be controlled. When you're angry, do you frequently yell or use physical force? If someone cuts you off while you're driving, do you holler out the window or make obscene gestures? If you're tired and frustrated after work, do you kick the dog or act short-tempered with your kids? If you want your kids to shun violence and learn peaceful ways to resolve conflicts, you'll first need to lead by example. Let your kids see you using alternatives to bad-mouthing or fighting to work out disagreements.

WHAT TO SAY ABOUT VIOLENCE IN OUR WORLD

When you want to talk about violence, you won't have to search far for a teachable moment. Unfortunately, each day gives us examples of the violence all around us. The following situations will give you an idea of how to use the world we live in to talk to your teenagers about violence.

Talk About Violent TV Shows and Movies

Popular media is violent. The American Psychological Association tells us that before a typical adolescent graduates elementary school he will have witnessed approximately eight thousand murders and one hundred thousand violent acts on TV. He will witness an additional ten thousand murders in the media by the end of high school. This exposure to television violence was the subject of a 1998 national study funded by the National Cable Television Association. This $3.5 million study of more than six thousand hours of television on twenty-three channels found that about one-third of all violent programs featured bad characters who weren't punished, 71 percent of violent scenes showed no remorse or criticism, and roughly half of violent shows showed no physical injury or pain on the victims' part. Nearly 40 percent of violence was instigated by good characters.

When violence is glamorized and sanitized this way, it becomes dangerously seductive and creates three problems for teenagers:

Mimicking: "Shut up, you brat, or I'll rip your head off!"
TV and movie violence teaches that aggression is a preferred way to resolve conflicts. Violent scenes provide step-by-step scripts that teach our kids how to react to anger. Research has found that children who watch too many violent shows are more likely to argue, disobey, and get into fights. They also tend to have weak problem-solving skills. These are the people with whom our teens share the world.

Desensitization: "Man, look at that blood gush out of his head. That's great!"

A casual attitude toward TV and movie violence creates the impression that aggression and hostile acts are commonplace and acceptable. When this happens, we stop feeling empathy for others' pain. We don't try to prevent violent acts and are slow to react to others' suffering. Violence no longer shocks us.

Exaggerated fear: "I'm afraid to take the garbage out at night. Somebody might jump me."

On TV and in movies, the world is a hostile, unsafe place. This view of life can result in what Dr. George Gerbner, of the University of Pennsylvania, calls the *mean world syndrome*. This is the belief that crime and violence are pervasive parts of our world. Gerbner believes that kids don't have enough real-world information to put what they see on TV and in the movies into perspective. They are likely to overestimate their chances of encountering violence and to believe their neighborhoods are unsafe, whether or not they actually are.

You can reduce the impact of media violence on your teens starting today right in your own home. Take a close look at what has become acceptable entertainment in your household. TV and other media violence is everywhere we turn, but that doesn't mean you have to be swept along with the crowd and accept it with open arms. You still have the right to monitor your teen's intake of violence.

Teenagers should be given the independence they need to learn how to make responsible decisions. But if your teen is immersed in violent entertainment, she is making wrong decisions, and it's your place to step in and say no. "No, I don't want you to watch that show." "No, you can't go to that movie." Sure, your teen will scream bloody murder (excuse the violent expression), but that will give you more teachable moments to talk about violence in our society.

If you know the facts before you put your foot down, you'll be better prepared to show your kids why you're limiting their daily dose of violence.

If your teen says: "Violent movies aren't anything new. You watched them when you were young."
You say: "The violence of *Bonnie and Clyde* is tame compared with the violence in movies today. In her book *Violence and the Media,* Victoria Sherrow gives us these body counts: *Total Recall* (81 dead); *Robocop 2* (106 dead); *Rambo III* (264 dead); *Die Hard 2* (64 dead), and *Natural Born Killers* (50 dead). Watching so much human misery for fun makes it difficult for us to feel horror over real human suffering."

If your teen says: "It's not violent."
You say: "Let's define 'violent.' I say it's physical force meant to harm or kill another person or damage or destroy property. What do you say it is?"

Faced with this factual definition, your teen may have to give you this one, but not necessarily. She may have her own definition that will give you insight into why the two of you disagree about the level of violence in the media.

If your teen says: "Violent TV shows and movies don't make people violent."

You say: "That's not what the facts say. An obvious example occurred in 1991 when the film *Boyz N the Hood* opened nationwide. The following incidents of violence followed:

In a Chicago suburb, a man was fatally shot after a midnight showing.

Five people were wounded in or near a large theater complex in Universal City, California.

In Sacramento, a nineteen-year-old woman was shot six times during a fight outside a theater.

In Tuscaloosa, Alabama, three teens were shot in a gang fight at a theater.

In Commack, New York, a teenager was stabbed by two attackers in the lobby of a theater.

"Other examples are all over the news: in New York City, a group of teenagers who set fire to a homeless man claimed they saw the act done on television. During a National Public Radio interview in 1993, a teenage gang member said that after watching *The Terminator* several times, he and his friends were 'pumped up,' eager to be like the unbeatable 'futuristic killing machine' in that film.

"Violent TV shows and movies *do* stimulate people to do violent things."

There may be an occasional blockbuster movie that absolutely "everyone" is going to see, and saying no to your teen will cause him to be ridiculed or otherwise demeaned by his friends. You'll have to use your judgment and make decisions on a case-by-case basis. But let your kids know that as a general rule, violence is not entertainment.

When your teen does watch a violent TV show or movie, use the situation as an opportunity to talk about violence and fantasy versus reality. To begin a discussion, you might use these conversation starters. Ask your teen:

"Do you like to watch violent shows?"
"Can you tell me how the violence acted out for 'entertainment' is different from violence in the world?"
"Do you think watching violence in movies makes a person more likely to become violent?"
"Do you think the violence in this movie is there to make a point or is it simply gratuitous?"

You can also use violent episodes to teach critical viewing skills. These skills help all of us separate what's real from what's not. Ask questions like these:

"Can that really happen?"
"How long do you think it took the makeup artist to apply that much blood to that actor?"
"If you were the script writer, would you have written that scene any differently?"
"Do you think it's good to make violent scenes look realistic?"

These kinds of questions remind your kids that what they're watching is not reality.

Talk About Violence in Video Games
Many experts feel that playing violent video games has a greater impact on a teen's desensitized reaction to violence than the passive acts of TV and movie watching. Kids playing video games take

an active role in enacting violence in very realistic, lifelike scenes and situations. They actively strive to maim, kill, injure, decapitate, and so on. And there is no consequence for these acts, no moral of the story, no good guy as the hero. There is no regard for human life. Sure, there have been cops-and-robbers games since you were kids, but these games are very different. Today's sophisticated computer graphics make each shootout look very realistic. The cries of pain and horror, the blood and guts are much more realistic than we could have dreamed.

Take a look at your kids' video games. If you don't like what you see, get rid of them. Trash the ones that make heroes out of cold-blooded killers and offer to replace them with games of challenge and competition. No doubt your kids will scream, and they'll still play the games at their friends' homes, but your overall goal is to take a stand, make a statement against violence, and reduce the amount of time your kids spend being desensitized.

Before you storm the video game closet, talk to your kids. Ask them for their opinion. Even though you can be pretty sure they'll tell you that "it's only for fun," that it's "not really violent," and that "everybody plays these games," give them a chance to talk. Talking out loud about the violence in front of them can open their eyes to the fact that violence should not be fun.

If your teen says: "Why can't I play these games?"
You say: "I know these games are very popular and everybody plays them, so I can understand why you feel you should be able to also. But that doesn't change the fact that graphic violence should not be considered entertainment. I would not expect to find anyone using these games at school or at the library because they're violent and unacceptable. I'm certainly not going to have them in my home."

If your teen says: "But why?"

You say: "I don't like the message that game sends. It makes violence seem like fun. I know other kids' parents let them play this game, but I don't want it played in my house."

Talk About Violent Lyrics in Music

An unacceptably large percentage of today's popular music contains messages of suicide, murder, assaults, death, personal gratification, thrill seeking, and the use of illegal drugs. Many music videos (specifically certain videos for rap music) are purposefully glorifying armed violence and criminality. Some demean women or describe graphic violence against them. All this is in the name of entertainment. You cannot stop teenagers from listening to popular music or watching music videos; these things are an inescapable part of their world. But don't throw up your hands completely—you still have some influence.

Be aware. Pay attention to the kind of music your kids like and listen to the lyrics. You should know which groups are known for gore and violence. (Ask your kids; they'll probably tell you, because part of the fun is knowing you hate it.) When buying birthday and holiday gifts, refuse to buy objectionable music and explain why. Tell your teens:

"I know you like this, but I really don't. I'm hoping the world you grow up into will be peaceful and kind to you. This kind of music makes too many young kids think that violence and abuse is the acceptable way to get what we want or settle our differences. I'm not going to give my money to support this kind of message. I hope that when you think about what your money supports when you purchase this, you'll think twice too."

If objectionable songs come on the radio when you're in the kitchen or driving the car, turn them off. When your kids complain, they give you another opportunity to explain your view about violent lyrics. Tell your teens:

"In my car [my house], I won't listen to music that glorifies violence. If your generation thinks violence is entertaining, you will never be able to walk the streets without fear."

When your teens protest that you're being crazy (and they will), encourage them to convince you that what they want to listen to is good. Ask them:

"What is the message of this song?"
"What's good about that?"
"Defend it. Convince me."

It is very unlikely that these conversations will end with your teen saying, "You're right. I'm never going to listen to that group again." But talking about violence in lyrics will help your teen sort out what's good and right from what's bad and wrong. That's what today's teens so often seem to lack: a clear view of right and wrong. Raunchy music lyrics give you the perfect opportunity to talk about subjects that otherwise might never come up.

Talk About Violence in the News

Violence is not only in the fantasy world of TV shows, movies, music, and videos. It is a real part of life. This is obvious every time we pick up a newspaper or magazine or turn on the radio or TV news. Murders, kidnappings, child abuse, rapes, assaults, domestic violence, alcohol- and drug-related crimes, hate crimes, muggings, hostage taking, riots, bombings, assassinations, snipers, gang violence, school violence, and racial and ethnic violence are as much a part of our daily lives in this society as brushing our teeth. If this isn't enough to make the world look like a scary place, we have TV talk shows that portray real-world violence as entertainment. Shocking topics, often involving sex and violence, bring us victims of assaults, rape, child abuse, spousal abuse, and other crimes. Victims and attackers tell their stories in loud, obscene language that often evolves into physical assaults. What is your teen supposed to think? Violence is unavoidable? Violence is funny? Uncontrolled violence defines the human spirit?

We believe that real-life violence has an even stronger impact on the way we view our world than TV shows and movies because people more readily interpret it as a true picture of the world. After an hour of the evening news, your teen can't say, "Oh, Mom, that doesn't really happen." You both know it does. The key problem with this reality is that a constant stream of violent images and stories can desensitize people. Feelings of shock and outrage decrease as violence becomes routine. Crime reporting begins to take on the distant and unreal quality of movie entertainment.

When possible, don't watch the evening news when your kids are around the TV. Use the newspaper and radio for discussions of current events, but try to limit daily intake of graphic viewing. When you do hear news reports together, use the time as an opportunity to talk to your teens about violence. When you hear a news story on the radio while driving in the car or having your morning coffee, talk about the event and your reactions. Conversation starters include the following:

"Did you hear that? How do you think those people feel?"

"Why would a person do such a thing?"

"Do you think that kind of thing could happen in our neighborhood? How does that make you feel?"

"Why do you think people are so full of anger?"

"Does that news shock you?"

"Do you think people lose the feeling of shock and horror when they read a news account of violence because they watch so much 'entertainment' violence?"

We may not be able to convince TV news producers to focus on the positive side of life (which is out there!), but at least negative news gives us an opportunity to talk to our teens about a fact of life.

Talk About Violence in School

Schools are no longer safe havens. The rash of mass murders inside schools in the 1997–98 school year proved that to the entire nation. Within a five-month period, a fourteen-year-old boy was charged with shooting and killing three students at a school in West Paducah, Kentucky; a fourteen-year-old was accused of firing from nearby woods and wounding two students in a school in Stamps, Arkansas; a sixteen-year-old boy in Mississippi was charged with killing his mother and then shooting nine students; and as noted at the start of this chapter, a thirteen-year-old and his eleven-year-old cousin ambushed students at Westside Middle School in Jonesboro, Arkansas, killing four young girls and one teacher. These kinds of horrific acts are not the only kind of violence in our schools. Many students routinely carry such weapons as guns, knives, brass knuckles, and razor blades to protect themselves. Many schools now have metal detectors at the doors and security guards patrolling the halls. All these things affect the way kids feel about their world. Help your teen talk about how he feels about violence in schools.

Ask your teen: "I read in the paper that kids bring guns to school because they feel they need protection. Do you think that's true?"

Ask your teen: "Do you feel safe in school?"
If the answer is no: "What would need to happen to make you feel safe?"

Ask your teen: "Do you think most kids think violence solves problems?"
If the answer is yes: "Why do you think they feel that way?"

Ask your teen: "What would you do if someone threatened you with violence in school?"

Talk About Guns

Crime reports tell us that every day fourteen children ages nineteen and under are killed in gun accidents, suicides, and homicides; many more are wounded. They also say that one hundred thousand students carry guns to school each day. Obviously, kids with guns are an escalating problem that can't be ignored.

Many teens feel packing a gun is necessary for protection in a world they see as hostile and dangerous. Peer pressure and curiosity also play a role. Also at fault is the easy availability of guns and the acceptance of guns in our society through messages conveyed in our culture, particularly in movies and TV. Kids think that carrying a gun will make others afraid of them and give them the upper hand.

Combine these factors with teens' impulsive nature, and the rise in gun violence committed by teenagers is not really surprising.

You need to take a firm stand against gun use by teenagers. Make sure your teen knows that he is never to have a gun or fool around with someone else's gun. Say:

"Stay away from guns. It's against the law."

Most states have laws forbidding the sale of guns to anyone under eighteen. The laws also forbid anyone of any age to carry a concealed weapon without a permit.

It would not be farfetched to imagine your teen in a situation where a friend suddenly reveals he or she has a gun. Before that happens, tell your teen:

"I want to go over with you what you need to do to stay safe if a friend ever shows you a gun. It's common for guns to go off when they're being shown off. You have two choices: (1) leave or (2) insist your friend put the gun away immediately."

If your teen asks: "Why are you so worried?"
You say: "The leading cause of death among teenagers is gunshot wounds."

If your teen asks: "Why shouldn't I carry a gun to school when everybody else does?"
You say: "For starters, it's against the law for someone your age to carry a gun. Also, carrying a gun puts you in very real danger. There are smarter ways to impress your friends and take care of yourself than carrying a gun that has only one real purpose: to kill."

If you have a gun in your house, don't assume your teen knows it's off-limits. Say so loud and clear. Store guns unloaded and locked up. Lock ammunition in a separate place.

Talk About Violent Love Relationships

What psychologists call low-level or noninjurious physical aggression between romantic partners is not cute. Partners who exchange insults, raised fists, shoving, or slaps in the face often find that the situation escalates into outright battering. A recent article presented by the American Psychological Association found low-level aggressive behavior particularly prevalent among high school and college students. They found that 20 to 50 percent of adolescents experience some form of violent behavior from a dating partner by the time they reach age fifteen. But the researchers were shocked to find that many couples regard such actions as innocuous, even normal in any loving relationship.

You can help your teens understand that violent actions are not a part of a loving relationship. Just talking about this subject can reduce their acceptance of dating violence and make them less tolerant of physical abuse in romantic arguments. Unless you see evidence that your teen is being physically abused in a relationship, it's probably best to talk in general about this subject. Otherwise, you imply that his or her dating partner is violent—a sure turn-off to further conversation. Say:

> "I've recently read that many teenage couples slap and push each other around when they're angry. Do you see that happening with your friends?"
>
> "I think that all teenagers need to know that love should never hurt. Dominating and jealous behaviors are not a sign of love."

"Anyone—teen or adult—who is slapped around by someone
he or she loves is being set up for a more serious battering.
People in this situation should end the relationship and look
for someone who loves them with respect."

You can get the free brochure "Love Doesn't Have to Hurt
Teens" from the American Psychological Association by calling
(202) 336-6046. This booklet will give you tips on how you can off-
set violent actions and attitudes before they become habit.

WHAT TO SAY ABOUT SOLVING CONFLICTS

Reducing the violence in society happens one person at a time—
start with your teen by helping him learn how to solve conflicts without violence. Of course, your example is a most powerful teacher, but
in addition, teach conflict resolution skills in your home.

Set firm limits regarding your children's actions toward each
other. If you tolerate siblings who yell and scream to vent their anger
or who hit to solve problems, you give the message that violence is
the way to get what you want. This message is the reason so many
kids feel free to use knives and guns to take a coat they want right
off the back of a classmate. This is not an extreme example. Kids
learn in the home how to get what they want. Tell your teens:

"In this house we do not solve problems with violence. You can
solve it yourself by talking it out, or you can ask me to be a mediator
who will listen to both sides and make a decision. If you decide to
fight, you will both be punished." (Make sure the punishment is
nonviolent—being grounded or having to clean out the garage
should do it.)

When your teens are involved in a conflict that begins to escalate, ask them to think: "What would happen if you tried to talk out a solution? What would happen if one of you just walked away?"

Talk about how these solutions work in everyday life. Talk about the adult world where you can't solve problems with your boss or your spouse by hitting. How are these problems solved? That's what your teens have to learn to do also.

Your teen may ask: "What if somebody hits me first?"
This is a tough one to answer because no one wants a child to be picked on. But your response will affirm your belief in nonviolent solutions.
You might say: "If somebody hits you first, I understand that you're going to be really angry and want to hit back. But you have to think about what hitting back will solve. You hit him, he hits you, and on and on, but the problem remains. Usually, violence causes more violence. But you can try to break that chain by walking away. It takes much more courage to do that than to strike back. If you walk away, you can have time to cool off and think of a nonviolent solution."

If your child needs some proof that this method works, you might have a conversation about Martin Luther King or Gandhi. Both led nonviolent revolutions and won.

WHAT TO SAY ABOUT AVOIDING VIOLENCE

Part of being safe in a violent society is being aware of the dangers and knowing how to avoid them. Go over the following list with your kids to make sure they know how to stay away from danger.

- Don't put yourself in danger.
- Don't take shortcuts through alleys.
- Don't wander in isolated areas.
- Don't be out alone after dark.
- Don't look like a victim.
- Always walk with confidence at a quick pace.
- If someone attacks or confronts you, yell "Fire!" This will draw people's attention. Yelling "Help!" often sends people running the other way.
- If attacked, fight back. Go for vulnerable areas such as eyes, groin, and throat, and use any weapons you can reach.
- If you think you're being followed, go to the nearest house with a light on, or go into an open place of business.
- When driving at night, keep doors locked and windows rolled up.
- Check inside and under your car before getting in after it has been parked.
- If you are followed when driving, don't go home. Drive to the nearest police station.
- Avoid gangs, even loosely knit groups with nothing to do. Many times groups form spontaneously out of boredom and begin what has been called *wilding*. The term was first used to identify the actions of seven teenage boys who were arrested for assaulting and raping a young woman in New York in 1989. These teens were wandering around with nothing to do and committed this violent act for the fun of it. Hanging out can turn dangerous.
- If you know that someone is considering violence, tell someone who can help. It's easier to prevent a dangerous situation than to survive one. The young boy in Alabama who shot and killed his classmates during a fire drill had told some friends that he was

going to do this. Maybe if one of those friends had told an adult, the outcome would have been very different.

WHAT TO SAY WHEN VIOLENCE STRIKES

If your teen has been directly involved in a violent act, whether as a victim or a witness, he or she needs lots of ongoing love, comfort, and assurances—and time to talk about the occurrence. Talking is often the best medicine for the psychological trauma of violence, so encourage your teen to talk about what happened. Then listen. Give your teen your full attention without giving your opinion or expressing your own anger. Simply say, "Tell me how you feel about that." Let your teen verbalize the fears that may be festering with no way out.

Don't worry that talking about a violent episode is like reliving it. Talking gives emotional release and lifts the burden of having to face the fear of violence alone. If your teen refuses to talk, give her space for now, but keep giving her opportunities to open up when the time is right.

Each form of violence requires a unique dialogue that can't be scripted here. But if you find that you simply don't know what to say to your child, don't hesitate to ask for help for both of you. When students experience the death of a classmate or an incidence of violence on school grounds, most schools immediately bring in counselors to help the teens deal with their upset feelings. Professional help is a smart option. You might start with the school counselor or ask the school for a referral to a trauma psychologist in your area.

You should also consider psychological counseling if your teen shows any of these behaviors:

Anxiety attacks
Chronic depression
Difficulty concentrating
No emotional response
Nightmares
Phobias

Professional counseling can help teens avoid posttraumatic stress syndrome, which makes it almost impossible to leave the incident behind and move on with life.

WHAT TO SAY WHEN YOUR TEEN IS THE PERPETRATOR

It is important to talk to our kids about the effect that violence has on their lives, but what do we say when you find out that it's your teen who is guilty of a violent action? What do you say when the phone call comes from the school saying that your teen started a fight, or your teen pulled a fire alarm, or your teen threatened a student or teacher with bodily harm? Your reaction should come in four steps:

1. *Find out what happened.* Although you may be very angry, always give your teen an opportunity to explain. Find out what happened and why.

2. *Emphasize empathy.* Talk to your teen about the effect of his actions on others. Ask him: "How do you think the other person felt when you did that?" "Put yourself in the other person's shoes; how would you react to what you did?" By instilling concern, caring, and empathy in your teen, you can help him see why violence is not a solution.

3. *Explain the consequences.* Whatever the reason for a violent action, your teen must hear you say, without hesitation, that violence in any form is not acceptable. Period. Make it clear that there are consequences for this kind of behavior. Don't brush off any violent action with a weak warning. Make your teen know that violence is never an acceptable solution and that there is always a price to pay. Whatever your family discipline code calls for (maybe grounding, yard work, or total restriction of computer and video games), make the punishment match the crime in severity. Tell your teen: "We all are held accountable for our actions in life. You have to accept responsibility for what you have done and face the consequences."

4. *Make amends.* Part of taking responsibility for mistakes is learning to make amends. Help your teen decide how the situation can be remedied. Ask your teen:

"Do you think an apology is appropriate?"

"Can you think of a way to fix the damage you've done?"

"Is there some action you can take now that will make up for your behavior?"

THE DIFFICULT TASK

The government and the media industries are all taking small steps toward reducing the presence of violence in daily life. They're trying program labeling, V-chips, FCC rules, and congressional hearings. Certainly, all this is better than nothing, but still the violence continues.

Many say it's a parent's responsibility to monitor a teen's viewing habits. We ask, is it possible to screen virtually very aspect of media influence? We can check the ratings on movies and read the labels on CDs, but can we find out if MTV and violent video games are allowed in every house in the neighborhood? Can we always be there when regular TV programming is interrupted for a live broadcast of a nearly naked man shooting himself in the head on a freeway in Los Angeles (which just happened this week as we were writing this chapter)?

The task is a difficult one. But by talking with our teens about the negative impact of all violence, we take a first and most important step. The world is telling them that violence is fun and normal; they need to hear their parents' assurances that it is not. The world is telling them that this is all there is; they need to hear from you that they do not have to take what is offered. Tell them: "You vote for the kind of world you want to live in every time you go to the box office, turn on the TV and radio, and make a purchase at the music store. Choose carefully."

We take a second important step every time we talk to our kids with respect. Say things that convey acceptance, appreciation, approval, admiration, and affection. Kids who get these things from their parents are not filled with the kind of anger that unleashes itself on society.

RESOURCES

Center for Conflict Resolution
200 N. Michigan Avenue, Suite 500
Chicago, IL 60601
(312) 372-6420

Institute for Mental Health Initiatives
Channeling Children's Anger
4545 42nd Street N.W., Suite 311
Washington, DC 20016
(202) 364-7111

National Crime Prevention Council
1700 K Street, 2nd floor
Washington, DC 20006
(202) 466-6272

National School Safety Center
4165 Thousand Oaks Boulevard, Suite 290
Westlake Village, CA 91362
(805) 373-9977

Center to Prevent Handgun Violence
1400 K Street N.W., Suite 500
Washington, DC 20005

The Family Violence and Sexual Assault Institute (FVSAI)
1310 Clinic Drive
Tyler, TX 75701
(903) 595-6600

FOR FURTHER READING

Sherrow, Victoria. *Violence and the Media*. Brookfield, Conn.: Millbrook Press, 1996.

Especially for Teens
Hyde, Margaret, and Elizabeth Forsyth. *The Violent Mind*. New York: Franklin Watts, 1991.

Leone, Bruno (ed.). *Youth Violence*. San Diego, Calif.: Greenhaven Press, 1992.

Miller, Maryann. *Coping with Weapons and Violence in Your School and on Your Streets*. New York: Rosen Publishing Group, 1993.

Chapter Notes

Introduction

Goodstein, Laurie, and Marjorie Connelly. "Teen-Age Poll Finds a Turn to the Traditional." *New York Times*, Apr. 30, 1998, p. A20.

Rhule, Patty. "Teens Tackle Their Identity Crisis." *USA Weekend*, May 1, 1998, pp. 6–7.

Death of a Loved One

Kübler-Ross, Elisabeth. *Death: The Final Stage of Growth*. New York: Simon & Schuster, 1986.

Date Rape

Giarrusso, R., and others. "Adolescent Cues and Signals: Sex and Sexual Assault." Paper presented at a symposium of the meeting of the Western Psychological Association, San Diego, Calif., Apr. 1979.

Hughes, Jean, and Bernice Resnick Sandler. *"Friends" Raping Friends*. Washington, D.C.: Center for Women Policy Studies, 1991.

Alcohol and Drinking and Driving

Mothers Against Drunk Driving. "Public Policy Statistics: Research on Youth." [http://www.madd.org/stats/stat_youth.shtml].

Mothers Against Drunk Driving. "Public Policy Statistics: The Impaired Driving Problem." [http://www.madd.org/stats/default.shtml].

Mothers Against Drunk Driving. "Under 21: Drinking and Driving." [http://www.madd.org/UNDER21/youth_issues.shtml].

U.S. Department of Health and Human Services. *Tips for Teens About Alcohol*. Washington, D.C.: U.S. Department of Health and Human Services, n.d.

Dangers on the World Wide Web
"Is Your Kid Caught Up in the Web?" *Consumer Reports*, May 1997, pp. 27–31.

Trebilcock, Bob. "Child Molesters on the Internet." *Redbook*, Apr. 1997, pp. 101–102, 136–137.

Drug Abuse
Manatt, Marsha. *Parents, Peers and Pot*. DHHS Publication No. (ADM) 80-812. Rockville, Md.: National Institute on Drug Abuse, 1980.

National Institute on Drug Abuse. *Peer Pressure: It's OK to Say No*. DHHS Publication No. (AADM) 83-1271. Rockville, Md.: National Institute on Drug Abuse, 1983.

National Clearinghouse for Alcohol and Drug Information. *Just the Facts*. Publication No. RP0884. Rockville, Md.: National Clearinghouse for Alcohol and Drug Information, n.d.

Regents of the University of Wisconsin and the National PTA. *Young Children and Drugs: What Parents Can Do*. Madison: Wisconsin Clearinghouse, 1984.

U.S. Department of Education. *Growing Up Drug Free: A Parent's Guide to Prevention*. Washington, D.C.: U.S. Department of Education, n.d.

U.S. Department of Health and Human Services. *Tips for Teens About Marijuana*. Washington, D.C.: U.S. Department of Health and Human Services, n.d.

U.S. Department of Health and Human Services. *Tips for Teens About Smoking*. Washington, D.C.: U.S. Department of Health and Human Services, n.d.

Sex, Contraception, and Pregnancy

Greydanus, Donald. *Caring for Your Adolescent: Ages 12 to 21*. New York: Bantam Books, 1991.

Padawer, Ruth. "Survey: Teens Want More Sex Information—They Say They Learn Some Facts Too Late." *Bergen Record*, June 25, 1996, p. A-19.

Warzak, William, and others. "Enhancing Refusal Skills: Identifying Contexts That Place Adolescents at Risk for Unwanted Sexual Activity." *Journal of Developmental and Behavioral Pediatrics*, Apr. 1995, pp. 98–100.

Sexually Transmitted Diseases

Brodman, Michael, and others. *Straight Talk About Sexually Transmitted Diseases*. New York: Facts on File, 1993.

Elkind, David. *Parenting Your Teenager*. New York: Ballantine, 1993.

U.S. Department of Health and Human Services. *Condoms and Sexually Transmitted Disease . . . Especially AIDS*. HHS Publication No. FDA 90-4239. Washington, D.C.: U.S. Department of Health and Human Services, n.d.

Tattoos and Body Piercing

Boudreau, John. "Teens' Penchant for Body Piercing Makes Parents, Lawmakers See Red." Knight-Ridder/Tribune News Service, Feb. 10, 1997, p. 210K3666.

Reybold, Laura. *Everything You Need to Know About the Dangers of Tattooing and Body Piercing*. New York: Rosen Publishing Group, 1996.

Teshima-Miller, Lani. "Getting a Tattoo." [rec.arts.bodyart: Tattoo FAQ2/9].

Competition

Avella, Douglas, and Theresa Foy DiGeronimo. *Raising a Healthy Athlete*. New York: British American Publishing, 1990.

Buckley, W.E.R., E. E. Yesalis, and K. K. Friedl. "Estimated Prevalence of Anabolic Steroid Use Among Male High School Seniors." *Journal of the American Medical Association*, 1988, 260, 3441.

Campbell, Laurie. "It's Only a Game." *Parent Paper,* Mar. 1996, p. 12.

Gleick, Elizabeth. "Every Kid a Star." *Time,* Apr. 22, 1996, pp. 39–40.

Women's Sports Foundation. "Myth Busting: What Every Female Athlete Should Know!"
[http://www.lifetimetv.com/WoSport/stage/RESLIB/mythbusting.html].

Cults

Langone, Michael. "Clinical Update on Cults." *Psychiatric Times,* July 1996, pp. 14, 16.

Pennsylvania Medical Society. "What Is a Cult?" *Pennsylvania Medicine,* July 1995.

Depression

National Center for Health Statistics. *Mortality Statistics.* Hyattsville, Md.: National Center for Health Statistics, 1993.

National Institute of Mental Health. *Helpful Facts About Depressive Illnesses.* DHHS Publication No. (ADM) 89-1536. Washington, D.C.: Alcohol, Drug Abuse, and Mental Health Administration, U.S. Department of Health and Human Services, 1987.

Smith, Tony, and Elizabeth Renwick. *Adolescence: The Survival Guide for Parents and Teenagers.* New York: DK Publishing, 1996.

Ethics, Moral Values, and Religion

Dosick, Wayne. *Golden Rules.* San Francisco: HarperSanFrancisco, 1995.

Mosedale, Laura. "Making Religion Relevant." *Child,* Jan. 1995, pp. 142–144, 172–175.

Segal, Julius. *Winning Life's Toughest Battles.* New York: Ivy Books, 1987.

Seligman, Martin E. P. *Learned Optimism.* New York: Knopf, 1991.

Seligman, Martin E. P., and others. *The Optimistic Child.* Boston: Houghton Mifflin, 1995.

Wright, Loyd S., and others. "Church Attendance, Meaningfulness of Religion, and Depressive Symptomatology Among Adolescents," *Journal of Youth and Adolescence*, 1993, *22*, 559–568.

Gangs

Chandler, Kathryn, and others. *Students' Reports of School Crime, 1989 and 1995*. NCES Survey Report No. 98241. Washington, D.C. National Center for Education Statistics, 1998.

National Crime Prevention Council. *A Parent's Guide for Preventing Gangs*. Washington, D.C.: National Crime Prevention Council, n.d.

National Crime Prevention Council. *Tools to Involve Parents in Gang Prevention*. Washington, D.C.: National Crime Prevention Council, 1992.

National Crime Prevention Council. *What's a Parent to Do About Gangs?* Washington, D.C.: National Crime Prevention Council, n.d.

Homosexuality

Bailey, J. M., and R. Pillard. "A Genetic Study of Male Sexual Orientation." *Archives of General Psychology*, 1991, *48*, 1089–1096.

Bailey, J. M., and others. "Heritable Factors Influence Sexual Orientation in Women." *Archives of General Psychology*, 1993, *50*, 217–223.

Bell, A. P., and others. *Sexual Preference: Its Development in Men and Women*. Bloomington: Indiana University Press, 1981.

Fighting the Myths: Lesbians, Gay Men—and Youth. New York: Hetrick-Martin Institute, 1993.

Garofalo, Robert, and others. "The Association Between Health Risk Behaviors and Sexual Orientation Among a School-Based Sample of Adolescents." *Pediatrics*, 1998, *101*, 895–902.

Gibson, P. "Gay Male and Lesbian Youth Suicide." *Report of the Secretary's Task Force on Youth Suicide*. Washington, D.C.: U.S. Department of Health and Human Services, 1989.

Hetrick, E. S., and A. D. Martin."Developmental Issues and Their Resolution for Gay and Lesbian Adolescents." *Journal of Homosexuality,* 1987, *14,* 25–43.

Kinsey, A. C., W. B. Pomeroy, and C. E. Martin. *Sexual Behavior in the Human Male.* Philadelphia: Saunders, 1948.

Kinsey, A. C., W. B. Pomeroy, and C. E. Martin. *Sexual Behavior in the Human Female.* Philadelphia: Saunders, 1953.

Klein, R. "Pride and Prejudice." *Times of London* Educational Supplement, June 6, 1997, p. TES2.

Remafedi, G. "Male Homosexuality: The Adolescent's Perspective." *Pediatrics,* 1987, *79,* 326–330.

Pornography

Osanda, Franklin Mark, and Sara Lee Johann. *Sourcebook on Pornography.* San Francisco: New Lexington Press, 1989.

Reisman, Judith. *"Soft Porn" Plays Hardball.* Lafayette, La.: Huntington House, 1991.

Prejudice

Edwards, Gabrielle. *Coping with Discrimination.* New York: Rosen Publishing Group, 1992.

National PTA and Anti-Defamation League of B'nai B'rith. *What to Tell Your Child About Prejudice and Discrimination.* New York: National PTA and Anti-Defamation League of B'nai B'rith, 1994.

Violence

American Psychological Association. *Violence and Youth: Psychology's Response: Summary Report of the American Psychological Association Commission on Violence and Youth.* Washington, D.C.: American Psychological Association, 1993.

Bureau of Justice Statistics, U.S. Department of Justice. "Criminal Victimization, 1996: Changes 1995–96 with Trends 1993–96." [http://www.ojp.usdoj.gov/bjs/abstract/cv96.htm].

Malloy, Richard. "Media Violations." *America*, Feb. 6, 1993, p. 4.

Moody, Kate. *Growing Up on Television: The TV Effect*. New York: Times Books, 1980; New York: McGraw-Hill, 1986.

Perkins, Craig. "Age Patterns of Victims of Serious Violent Crime." Bureau of Justice Statistics, U.S. Department of Justice, Publication No. NCJ-162031. [http://www.ojp.usdoj.gov/bjs/pub/ascii/apvsvc.txt], Sept. 1997.

Sherrow, Victoria. *Violence and the Media*. Brookfield, Conn.: Millbrook Press, 1996.

Sleek, Scott. "'Innocuous' Violence Triggers the Real Thing." *APA Monitor*, Apr. 1998, *29*, 1, 31.

Smith, Stacy L., and others. *National Television Violence Study*, Vol. 3. Washington, D.C.: National Cable Television Association, Apr. 1998.

The Authors

Charles E. Schaefer, Ph.D., is a professor of psychology and director of the Center for Psychological Services at Fairleigh Dickinson University. He is the author of many parenting books, including *How to Talk to Your Kids About Really Important Things* (with Theresa Foy DiGeronimo). Schaefer lectures widely across the country on parenting issues and has appeared on many TV shows as a child development expert.

Theresa Foy DiGeronimo, M.Ed., is adjunct professor of English and communications at William Paterson University of New Jersey and the mother of three children. She has written many books for parents, including the best-seller *Raising a Thinking Child* (with Myrna Shure).

OTHER BOOKS BY
CHARLES E. SCHAEFER and THERESA FOY DiGERONIMO

HOW TO TALK TO YOUR KIDS
ABOUT REALLY IMPORTANT THINGS
Charles Schaefer and Theresa Foy DiGeronimo
Jossey-Bass Inc., Publishers, 1994

GOOD KIDS/BAD HABITS
Charles Schaefer and Theresa Foy DiGeronimo
Random House/Crown, 1993

WINNING BEDTIME BATTLES
Charles Schaefer and Theresa Foy DiGeronimo
Carol Publishing, 1992

RAISING BABY RIGHT
Charles Schaefer and Theresa Foy DiGeronimo
Random House/Crown, 1992

HELP YOUR CHILD GET THE MOST OUT OF SCHOOL
Charles Schaefer and Theresa Foy DiGeronimo
New American Library, 1990

TEACH YOUR CHILD TO BEHAVE
Charles Schaefer and Theresa Foy DiGeronimo
New American Library, 1990

TOILET TRAINING WITHOUT TEARS
Charles Schaefer and Theresa Foy DiGeronimo
New American Library, 1989
Revised and updated, 1998

TEACH YOUR BABY TO SLEEP THROUGH THE NIGHT
Charles Schaefer and Michael Petronko
G.P. Putnam's Sons, 1987

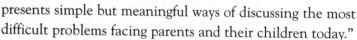